"If you lead a busy life and need a [...] going in the morning, check out Lo[...] a depth of biblical knowledge and in[...] reading for each of the sixty-six books of the Bible. [...] t! In just five minutes a day, you'll have a Bible story or concept to think about, a personal application for your life, and an action step to take. Buy one copy for yourself and ten more to give away."

CAROL KENT, speaker and author of *He Holds My Hand: Experiencing God's Presence & Protection*

"Are you looking for *more* in God's Word? While the Bible is filled with rich stories and ageless wisdom, too often we gravitate to the most familiar passages. Lori Hatcher helps us see truth in all of Scripture through her new devotional, *Refresh Your Faith: Uncommon Devotions from Every Book of the Bible*. What a treasure! Sixty-six days of mining hidden gems found in God's Word. Of course I love the stories, but I also appreciate the way Lori interacts with the reader and encourages us to dig deeper for our personal daily application. My own curiosity for further learning makes *Refresh Your Faith* a perfect daily guide. Highly recommended for anyone who loves to discover, digest thoroughly, and then act on faith."

LUCINDA SECREST MCDOWELL, author of *Life-Giving Choices* and *Dwelling Places*

"*Refresh Your Faith: Uncommon Devotions from Every Book of the Bible* is like journeying through the Bible on a treasure hunt every day. Lori Hatcher unearths nuggets from Scripture that are easy to overlook in a casual reading. This book inspires me to dig deeper for these hidden gems. Quite refreshing indeed!"

CARMEN ROBERSON, veteran Bible Study Fellowship (BSF) teaching leader

"I'm grateful for Lori's work on devotions to help refresh my memory on the beauty of the Bible and its stories of power, redemption, and ultimately the God who loves us. I know so many will walk away refreshed and more aware of the Father's love!"

KRISTI CLEMENTS, licensed professional counselor and
pastor's wife

"Lori Hatcher's unusual yet rich approach to this devotional book never runs roughshod over the revealed truth of God's Word. . . . It provides solid, exceptional biblical truth, practical guidelines, and refreshing depth."

DON L. MCCUTCHEON, Sr., DMin, former state director of
evangelism for the Baptist State Convention of North Carolina

"As longtime readers of the Bible and many devotional books, we enjoyed Refresh Your Faith by Lori Hatcher. Her writing is clear and applicable to real life, long enough to make a point that sticks with you for the day but short enough to read even on rushed days."

PASTOR AND MRS. DICK LINCOLN, Shandon Baptist Church,
Columbia, South Carolina

"Theologically rich. Biblically deep. Practical. Insightful. Good stuff."

JOSH HUNT, author of *Good Questions Have Groups Talking Bible studies*

refresh
your
faith

refresh
your
faith

uncommon
devotions
from every book
of the Bible

Lori Hatcher

Our Daily Bread
Publishing™

Requests for permission to quote from this book should be directed to: Permissions Department, Our Daily Bread Publishing, PO Box 3566, Grand Rapids, MI 49501, or contact us by email at permissionsdept@odb.org.

Scripture quotations, unless otherwise indicated, are taken from the Holy Bible, New International Version®, NIV®. Copyright © 1973, 1978, 1984, 2011 by Biblica, Inc.™ Used by permission of Zondervan. All rights reserved worldwide. zondervan.com.

Scripture quotations marked HCSB are from the Holman Christian Standard Bible®. Copyright © 1999, 2000, 2002, 2003, 2009 by Holman Bible Publishers. Used by permission. Holman Christian Standard Bible®, Holman CSB®, and HCSB® are federally registered trademarks of Holman Bible Publishers.

Scripture quotations marked NKJV are from the New King James Version®. Copyright © 1982 by Thomas Nelson. Used by permission. All rights reserved.

Interior design by Angela Messinger

Library of Congress Cataloging-in-Publication Data

Names: Hatcher, Lori, author.
Title: Refresh your faith : uncommon devotions from every book of the Bible / Lori Hatcher.
Description: Grand Rapids, MI : Our Daily Bread Publishing, 2020. | Includes bibliographical references. | Summary: "Build your faith with 66 culturally relevant, story-driven devotions that spotlight unfamiliar passages from every book of the Bible. Be challenged to think about things you've never thought about before"-- Provided by publisher.
Identifiers: LCCN 2019046755 (print) | LCCN 2019046756 (ebook) | ISBN 9781640700079 (paperback) | ISBN 9781640700598 (ebook)
Subjects: LCSH: Bible--Meditations.
Classification: LCC BS491.5 .H377 2020 (print) | LCC BS491.5 (ebook) | DDC 242/.5--dc23
LC record available at https://lccn.loc.gov/2019046755
LC ebook record available at https://lccn.loc.gov/2019046756

Printed in the United States of America

20 21 22 23 24 25 26 27 28 / 8 7 6 5 4 3 2

To my grandchildren, Lauren, Caroline, Andrew, and Collin.
May you always love God's Word.

Contents

Contents

The Inspiration behind
Refresh Your Faith

I'll never forget the first time I read the story of Jonah. As a new believer, I couldn't stop thinking about it. The same thing happened when I read the story of Moses parting the Red Sea. And Daniel's sleepless night in the lions' den. The stories inspired and fascinated me. But after a while, something changed. The fabulous stories became familiar. Their knockout punches became more like gentle pats—comforting, but certainly not seismic. To fight the boredom that threatened to lull me into spiritual sleep, I bought several women's devotionals. Sadly I discovered most authors seemed stuck in the same rut I was in. Their devotions focused on the same well-worn stories and verses I'd been reading in my own quiet times. *Zzzzzzz.*

Then I participated in a Bible study called *Let Prayer Change Your Life.* In one of the sessions, author and speaker Becky Tirabassi challenged us to read through the Bible in a year using *The One Year Bible.* As I began to read the *whole* Bible, not just the familiar sections to which I'd previously gravitated, I discovered books and passages I'd read but never really *seen* before.

Buried in familiar portions of the Bible and in obscure books like Ezra, Habakkuk, and Philemon were dynamic, life-changing verses. Before, I'd avoided or skimmed these less-familiar sections. Now their gems shined with extraordinary brilliance. In the more well-known books, I discovered unlikely verses that sparkled with truth and life application. Perhaps if others knew these gems were here, I thought, they'd fall in love with the Bible too.

This is how *Refresh Your Faith: Uncommon Devotions from Every Book of the Bible* was born.

It's my prayer that as you journey with me through little-known and often overlooked verses in every book of the Bible, you, too, will discover the joy, excitement, and riches of God's Word. I hope you'll not only fall in love with the Bible, you'll fall in love (or back in love) with God, the author of the Bible.

Two of the Most Important Questions

The LORD God called to the man, "Where are you?"

GENESIS 3:9

In Genesis 3:9 God asks one of the most important questions in the Bible.

Picture the scene. The paint was barely dry on God's creation masterpiece. In the pristine world, animals and humans lived in perfect harmony. Adam and his bride, Eve, were naked and unashamed. No sin corrupted their relationship with each other or with their Creator. God and the couple walked and talked together in the cool of the day.

That is . . . until Satan and his evil henchman, Sin, entered in. Satan lied to Eve and enticed Adam and Eve both to doubt God's goodness and disobey His instructions not to eat from one specific tree. From the first bite of toxic disobedience, Eve and her husband were naked and ashamed. They stitched pitiful faux coverings for themselves and hid in fear from God. Their once intimate relationship with Him was broken. In disgust and judgment God could and should have turned His back on them, but instead, He came calling. And He asked the question: "Where are you?" (Genesis 3:9).

His question to Adam is His question to us as well: *Where are you in relationship to me?*

Are we, like Adam and Eve, partially clothed with our own pitiful attempts to cover our sin? Hiding from Him because we've disobeyed His instructions and spurned His love? Or are we naked and unashamed, clothed in Christ's righteousness, and walking in sweet camaraderie and obedience with Him?

God's piercing question in the Old Testament can only be answered by a thorough understanding of the first question of the New Testament: "Where is *He*?"

"Now after Jesus was born in Bethlehem of Judea in the days of Herod the king, behold, wise men from the East came to Jerusalem, saying, 'Where is He who has been born King of the Jews?'" (Matthew 2:1–2 NKJV).

Does it really matter where we are in relationship to God unless we know where God is in relationship to us?

And where is He? He's right here, seeking us. "For the Son of Man"—that's Jesus—"came to seek and to save the lost" (Luke 19:10). God sent His Son Jesus into the world for a specific purpose: to seek you and me.

If you don't yet have a relationship with Christ, He wants you to know He's been there all along, pursuing you your whole life. He's eager to welcome you into His family. He invites you into fellowship with Him by settling His question to you: *Where are you?*

If you're ready to acknowledge His presence, He offers to save you from the penalty of your sins without you having to earn it or deserve it. "He saved us, not because of righteous things we had done, but because of his mercy" (Titus 3:5).

And once we accept Him as our Savior, He bestows upon us the wealth of His kingdom: forgiveness from sin, freedom from guilt, and a life filled with hope and peace. He promises to walk with us and live in us so we can face every trial that comes into our lives. If Christ is our Savior, He is close to the brokenhearted, with us wherever we go, and seated at the right hand of the Father, interceding on our behalf. He guides us and lives in us. Best of all, He eagerly waits to welcome us home to live with Him forever.

From the beginning of the Bible to the end, it's easy to see that God eagerly desires a relationship with us, one He offers freely to all who would receive Him.

Uncommon Thought
The two questions "Where are you?" and "Where is He?" prove God isn't distant or disinterested. He is there, pursuing you, loving you, and patiently waiting for you to acknowledge His presence and call out for Him.

Unusual Faith
As we begin this journey of sixty-six uncommon devotions, take a moment to ask yourself these two questions: Where am I in relationship to God? And where is God in relationship to me? Your honest answers will set the stage for an exploration into the depths of God's love for you.

Read Genesis 3:1–24.

Too Busy to Rest

"Three times a year all your men are to appear before
the Sovereign LORD, the God of Israel. I will drive out
nations before you and enlarge your territory, and no
one will covet your land when you go up three times
each year to appear before the LORD your God."

EXODUS 34:23–24

Most of us are driven people. Every day we feel the press to do and be
more. We must check off one more box on our to-do lists. We awaken
overwhelmed, and stumble into bed exhausted, mentally scrolling the
next day's list. Our work overflows into our nights and weekends, and
even when we're not working, we're not resting. There's always *one
more thing* calling us.

Sadly, this relentless press even threatens our time with the Lord.
Sunday—a sacred day set aside to worship God, rest, and spend time
with family—isn't sacred any longer.

The Lord knows our propensity to overwork. To protect against
this, He included the call to rest in the Ten Commandments and tucked a
special clause into His instructions to the Israelites in Exodus 34:23–24.

"Three times a year all your men are to appear before the Sovereign LORD, the God of Israel. I will drive out nations before you and
enlarge your territory, *and no one will covet your land* when you go up three

times each year to appear before the LORD your God" (emphasis mine). Do you see it? "No one will covet your land." God is saying, *Don't worry that your livelihood is going to suffer because you take time off to worship me. I'll protect and care for it. I'll watch over it while you do the right thing.*

This promise comforts me because sometimes the press of deadlines and the pile of work deceive me into thinking I don't have time for worship. That I don't have the luxury of a day off. That time digging in the dirt with my grandchildren or having dinner with friends is frivolous and presumptuous.

The truth is that God established a priority list we would do well to heed. It reads something like this:

1. Spend time with God first. Read your Bible every day. Pray. Worship together with other believers.
2. Work hard. Six days if necessary, but save the seventh one for the Lord.
3. Don't neglect time with your family.

Several Christian businesses in my town have demonstrated that we can have well-ordered biblical priorities and still succeed. They get it. They work hard six days a week, then they take the day off—to worship God, rest, and spend time with family. They believe God's promise that He'll watch over their businesses as they honor Him.

I'm glad God's promise doesn't just apply to large corporations or wealthy people. It also applies to you and me.

Uncommon Thought
When the press of deadlines and the pile of work deceive you into thinking you don't have time for rest and worship, God's Word says otherwise. He promises to watch over your livelihood as you honor Him.

Unusual Faith

Do you feel like you're too busy? Are you afraid to take a day off to honor the Lord, rest, and spend time with God and family? Has the promise of Exodus 34:23–24 helped change your thinking? Because God's Word is always true, you can claim it. Make a plan for next Sunday (and the Sunday after that, and the Sunday after that), and act upon it. Then watch God work. If Sunday work is mandatory in your job, brainstorm ways to worship, rest, and connect with family on another day.

Read Exodus 34:21–24.

Will God Really Provide?

"When you enter the land I am going to give you, the
land itself must observe a sabbath to the LORD. For
six years sow your fields, and for six years prune your
vineyards and gather their crops. But in the seventh year
the land is to have a year of sabbath rest, a sabbath to the
LORD. Do not sow your fields or prune your vineyards."

LEVITICUS 25:2–4

"Don't plant," God said.

Not, "Don't plant some of your fields," or, "Don't plant some of
your crops," but, "Don't plant anything at all."

Your family, your community, even your nation depends on you
to grow a crop that will feed them for an entire year. Like your parents
and their parents before them, your family has always made a living
from the soil. If you don't plant, you don't reap. If you don't reap, you
won't eat.

And God says, "Don't plant."

How would you feel? What would you say to God?

"Don't plant a crop, Lord? Are you crazy? How am I going to
feed my family?"

"Just for a year," the Lord says. "The land needs a rest, and you
do too."

"A *year*? If I don't plant for a year, then it will be *two* years before we harvest again. You know it takes an entire season to grow a crop."

"Do it anyway," the Lord says. "Trust me."

Then God took it even further. After seven sets of seven years had passed, forty-nine years in total, on the fiftieth year, God commanded the Israelites to celebrate the year of Jubilee. We read about it in Leviticus 25. Again the Lord called for a sabbath rest for the land. No sowing. No reaping. No farming of any kind.

But this time, because the year of Jubilee followed the standard seventh-year sabbath rest, God's command meant that the Israelites wouldn't plant for two consecutive years. And that it would be *three* years before they harvested a crop.

Observing this year of Jubilee required the Israelites to believe that God could and would provide for them. Totally and completely.

He anticipated their question: "What will we eat in the seventh year if we do not plant or harvest our crops?" (v. 20).

Listen to His response: "I will send you such a blessing in the sixth year that the land will yield enough for three years" (v. 21).

Do you hear what God is saying? "Trust me. Obey me. I will take care of you. Because you are faithful and obedient, I'm going to bless you so much that when the time of empty fields comes, you'll have enough to see you through."

Jesus shared the New Testament parallel to this Scripture: "Seek first his kingdom and his righteousness, and all these things"—everything you truly need—"will be given to you" (Matthew 6:33).

This principle of trusting God to provide for our needs as we obeyed His instructions should have been the plumb line by which my husband and I evaluated every major decision we made in our thirty years of marriage. Unfortunately, while we've always owned this objective standard, we haven't always pulled it out of our spiritual toolbox. Some days we measured our decision with the ruler of common sense. Or the yardstick of fear. Or the tape measure of self-protection. Other days, faith and obedience prevailed. We planted our mustard seed of faith, watered it with prayer, and watched God grow a miracle. These moments have been some of our grandest faith experiences:

- The anonymous donor who paid my husband's way through college when he obeyed God's call to go back to school.
- The way the hospital erased our bill when the Lord prompted us to try for another baby.
- The kind friend who gave us a computer when ours died, and we chose not to go into debt to buy another.
- The generous church family who donated money when my husband lost his job.
- And the family who obeyed the Lord's prompting to give us a financial gift—the day we received the news that our home needed thousands of dollars of repairs after South Carolina's historic one-thousand-year flood.

Our family is living proof that when Christians obey God, He will provide for them. We may not have everything we wish for, but God has always met our needs. Sometimes He provides even more than necessary, and other times He gives us exactly what we need to encourage us to trust Him. Even when we lack, we can trust God is at work.

Uncommon Thought

If you're reasonably certain the Lord is calling you to take a step of faith, even if it doesn't make sense, do it. By doing so, you'll plant tiny mustard seeds of faith that will sprout into a great harvest.

Unusual Faith

Is God calling you to obey Him, but you can't make the numbers add up? Is He calling you to quit your job and stay home with your children? Serve in a ministry that's way outside your comfort zone? Surrender to the mission field? Do what's right at work, even though it may cost you? Right a wrong, at personal expense? Pray hard, seek wise counsel, search God's Word for direction, and count the cost. Then step out in faith to obey Him.

Read Leviticus 25:1–22.

Misunderstandings and Hurt Feelings

"If we have found favor in your eyes," they said,
"let this land be given to your servants as our
possession. Do not make us cross the Jordan."

NUMBERS 32:5

I knew I was in trouble when my friend Marissa asked me when would be a good time to talk. "There's a matter I'd like to discuss with you privately," she said. A knot began to form in the pit of my stomach. The kind I used to get when the teacher asked me to stay after school. Turns out, I was in trouble. I had hurt Marissa's feelings and made her think I doubted her competency.

When she shared her concerns with me, I exclaimed, "That's not what I meant at all. Please let me explain." I filled in the backstory and told her what had prompted the action I'd taken. "I'm so sorry," I concluded. "You are one of the smartest women I know, and I would never intentionally hurt you. Will you please forgive me?"

She graciously forgave me, and our friendship emerged from the conflict stronger than it had ever been.

Marissa employed a wise biblical principle of conflict resolution when she asked to talk with me that day. We see another example of this in Numbers 32.

The children of Israel were preparing to cross the Jordan River into the promised land. They had waged a successful campaign against the Midianites and were surveying the rich pastureland they now commanded. The tribes of Reuben and Gad realized the land would be a perfect place to settle with their vast numbers of sheep and goats.

"Would it be okay if we settled on this side of the Jordan instead of going across with the rest of the Israelites?" they asked Moses.

Poor Moses, weary from trudging through forty years in the desert, didn't receive their request very well. He'd had to deal with a previous group of dissenters who hadn't wanted to go into the promised land.

"What do you mean, 'Would it be okay if we settled on this side of the Jordan?'" he asked. "Don't you remember what happened when the last generation didn't want to enter the land? If you don't go to battle with the other tribes, they'll grow fainthearted and discouraged. We'll never possess the land!"

"No, no, no," the Reubenites and Gadites replied. "That's not what we meant at all. We're more than happy to fight alongside our brothers. We'd just like to settle on this side of the river when the battles are over."

"Ahhhhhh," Moses said, "now I understand. Thanks for explaining."

Misunderstandings. They happen all the time. Sometimes we misspeak. Other times we misinterpret. We get incomplete information and draw a faulty conclusion. Once in a while, someone truly is rude or insensitive. Our feelings are hurt, and we get angry.

It doesn't matter how others offend us. What matters is how we handle it. Do we assume the worst and get mad? Do we replay the offense again and again in our minds, driving the knife deeper into our own punctured hearts? Do we talk about it to other people and receive comfort and justification from their reactions?

Or do we pursue peace and reconciliation? "If it is possible," Paul reminds us in Romans 12:18, "as far as it depends on you, live at peace with everyone."

Often this means initiating a meeting—as my friend Marissa did —expressing our feelings respectfully, and listening to the other's explanation. It means broaching the sore subject with the goal of restoration, not revenge. It means being willing to humble ourselves and take the first step toward reconciliation.

If my friend had taken my words at face value, been offended, stopped talking to me, and gossiped about my meanness, our friendship could have suffered a fatal blow. Instead, she responded to the offense with wisdom and maturity. She valued our relationship enough to pursue peace. Today, years later, she remains one of my dearest friends.

I'm grateful she made the effort to talk with me about our misunderstanding. I know she is too.

Uncommon Thought
Misunderstandings and offenses will happen. But when our goal is to restore the relationship, we'll listen well, admit when we're wrong, and do whatever's necessary to make amends.

Unusual Faith
Is there a damaged relationship in your life? Could the Lord be calling you to take the first steps toward reconciliation? Pray about it, then reach out to that person today.

Read Numbers 32.

DEUTERONOMY

One Reason God Says No

"I, the LORD your God,
am a jealous God."

DEUTERONOMY 5:9

Jealousy is a powerful thing.

Those who succumb to its green-eyed madness have made public spectacles of themselves, done things they've regretted later, and even committed crimes like assault and murder.

So why would God say, "I, the LORD your God, am a jealous God" (Deuteronomy 5:9)?

God's brand of jealousy is very different from human jealousy. We feel jealous when our husbands or boyfriends talk too long to other women. We struggle when our coworker gets the promotion we deserve. Or when we notice how terrific the neighbor looks since she lost all that weight. Human jealousy is self-focused.

We feel jealous because we feel threatened. We compare ourselves with the other woman, the ladder-climbing coworker, or the svelte lady next door and realize we don't measure up. We fear our well-being is in danger. Our jealousy, by nature, is rooted in self-preservation.

God's jealousy, however, rises from a different motive—our good and His glory.

God doesn't feel jealous because people pray to Buddha, Muhammad, or any of the thousands of gods in the world. He doesn't compare himself with pantheism and wish He'd thought to suggest people worship trees and nature. And He doesn't check His appearance and think, If I looked more appealing, people would love me more.

Instead of being self-focused, God's jealousy focuses on the well-being of those He loves—us.

He wants us to serve Him because He knows that true fulfillment comes from serving others, not from serving ourselves. He wants us to desire a relationship with Him, spend time in His presence, and share our hearts' desires with Him because He knows our lives will be better if we know Him intimately.

He wants us to follow Him because He knows wholehearted devotion gives our lives the right direction, God-directed purpose, and ultimate meaning. He wants us to love Him not because it's good for Him but because it's good for us. And when we love Him, we bring Him glory, which is mankind's highest calling.

Because God wants the best for us—the objects of His love—He jealously pursues us. He loves us unconditionally and forgives us every time we genuinely repent. And, oftentimes, He withholds those things that will compete with our loyalty and affection for Him. He protects us from what He knows will distract or hinder us from following Him wholeheartedly. Sometimes He says no to good things that stand in the way of His greater purpose.

We may think we're praying for good things. However, the good things we pray for could replace God in our lives. Sometimes even the *desire* for these good things can take God's place. We think if we could just find a husband (or get rid of the one we have), we'd be happy. Or have a child, get a promotion, or buy our dream home. We set that thing—whatever we've set our affection on—squarely on the throne of our lives.

And if something else is on the throne, guess who's not? And here's a frightening thought—many times we don't even realize that our desire for something good from God has displaced God himself.

Seventeenth-century scientist Blaise Pascal, in his book *Pensées*, described an "infinite abyss" in the heart of each man which cannot be satisfied by any created thing, but only by God himself. Because God knows we won't be truly happy until we find our satisfaction in Him alone, He jealously seeks to protect us from the good things that might distract us from what's best.

Uncommon Thought

Sometimes God says no to good things we pray for that stand in the way of His greater purpose for us.

Unusual Faith

Sometimes we want something so badly we forget that God and His will must come first. Today, if you're longing for something God hasn't granted yet, take a step back. Remember God's promise not to withhold anything good from you. Picture yourself holding the object of your desire in your hands. In a time of commitment and surrender, lift your hands to God and offer up that desire to the Lord.

Pray something like this:

Father, I deeply desire _____. But even more than
_____, I want you. Help me trust that if this desire is
from you and for my good, you'll bring it to pass in your

perfect timing. If this would harm me, hinder me, draw me away from you, or not best serve your greater purpose, I ask you to remove the desire from my heart. I surrender it to you today. Amen.

Read Deuteronomy 5:1–10.

JOSHUA

A Name Worthy of Respect

"Now give me this hill country that the LORD
promised me that day. You yourself heard then
that the Anakites were there and their cities
were large and fortified, but, the LORD helping
me, I will drive them out just as he said."
Then Joshua blessed Caleb son of Jephunneh
and gave him Hebron as his inheritance.

JOSHUA 14:12–13

I don't have a son, and the sons-in-law I've acquired came already
named. But if I had a son, I think I'd name him Caleb. Here are five
reasons why:[1]

1. *Caleb wasn't afraid of daunting tasks. He knew God would*
   help him.

Caleb was one of twelve spies who went into Canaan to scope out
the land as the children of Israel prepared to conquer it. All twelve
agreed the land was bountiful and "flowing with milk and honey."
But ten of the twelve were intimidated by the fortified cities and the
Anakites—a race of very tall and imposing people.

Caleb and his buddy Joshua had fearless faith. "Let's go in

immediately," they said. "The cities are strong, the people are large, but with God as our helper, we can conquer this land!"

2. *Caleb maintained his integrity. Even though he suffered due to others' sins, he stood by his values.*

Unlike Caleb, the Israelites were frightened and faithless. God punished their unbelief by making them wander in the wilderness until every person who said no to God had perished. Even the mighty patriarch Moses sinned and didn't get to enter the promised land. This left two men standing—Joshua and Caleb.

These men did everything right, but because of everyone else's sin, they had to wander and wait for thirty-eight years. But you know what? They kept their faith. They kept their integrity. They waited patiently, served their brothers, and continued to believe God was going to do what he'd promised.

3. *Caleb served faithfully in the shadow of another leader.*

It was promotion time. God told Moses he wasn't going into the promised land, so it was time to appoint a successor. There were only two candidates—Joshua and Caleb. Both were wise, godly, faithful, courageous men. God chose Joshua, and Caleb got passed over.

There's no injustice here. God knew who was most qualified to lead the Israelites. But don't you think Caleb felt a bit hurt and disappointed? I know I would.

How did he handle it? Throw a tantrum, howl about God's unfairness, take his camels and go back to Egypt? Nope. He kept serving the Lord. He supported Joshua, threw his wholehearted allegiance behind him, and continued to carry out his duties as a leader.

4. *Caleb went the distance.*

When the land was largely conquered, it was time for the Israelites to settle into their respective cities. But Caleb didn't grab a seat and rest. He grabbed his sword and kept going. He asked for land that was still occupied. Kenneth Gangel, in *Holman Old Testament Commentary: Joshua*, describes Caleb's unusual request:

> Even after eighty-five difficult years, Caleb had a great attitude
> about serving God and fighting for him. He wasn't tired out;
> in fact, he was just getting excited. He didn't walk up to his
> old buddy Joshua to ask for a maintenance-free, energy-saving
> home. . . . No, he asked for the hill country still inhabited by
> giants. He wanted the very area that had intimidated the other
> ten spies.[2]

I love this about Caleb. When he could have justifiably asked for an easy retirement, he asked instead for a daunting task he could only accomplish with God's help and enabling.

Caleb is an amazing man of God. I admire, respect, and want to emulate him. He's a man worthy of giving a son his name, don't you think?

Uncommon Thought
Despite suffering the consequences of other people's sins and being overlooked, Caleb served God and others courageously, clung to his integrity, and chose to do the harder things.

Unusual Faith

Are you walking through a difficult season of life right now? Are you suffering for someone else's sins, tempted to take the easy way out, or chafing under someone else's leadership? Or are you serving humbly and wholeheartedly like Caleb? Be honest with yourself and with God. Then ask God to give you the heart of Caleb. Ask Him to enable you not only to take on challenges but to seek them out for God's glory.

Read Joshua 14:6–14.

God of Wrath or God of Love?

And he could bear Israel's misery no longer.

JUDGES 10:16

"The God of the Old Testament is a God of wrath, not a God of love." The well-dressed man sitting across from me went on to say, "Time after time, He sent His 'chosen people,' Israel, into captivity instead of protecting them. He's fickle too. He'd rescue them when they cried out for help, then thirty years later, He'd allow another nation to come in and destroy them. I just can't trust a God who's so inconsistent."

It made me sad to realize that even though this man said he was a student of the Bible, he had apparently missed God's heart. I wondered if he had only read limited portions of the Old Testament, judging God without giving Him a fair chance.

Fifteen years ago I began reading the Bible through every year. This commitment led me into parts of Scripture I'd never read—difficult books of the Old Testament like Judges, Isaiah, and Jeremiah. I found most of the major and minor prophetic books full of warnings that God was going to bring judgment on Israel if they didn't repent of their sins and turn back to Him.

If all I'd read in those books were God's threats to destroy Israel, I'd probably agree that the God of the Old Testament (who is also the God of the New Testament) is a God of wrath. But for every warning of God's judgment on Israel, the prophets also recorded innumerable verses that spoke of God's patient and loving heart toward His people. Judges 10:11–16 is a perfect example.

Before we dig into this passage, let's consider the background. Time after time, the Israelites turned their backs on God and served the pagan idols of the surrounding nations. God allowed them to reap the consequences of their actions until they were horribly oppressed. They cried out to Him for deliverance, and He rescued them. They'd serve God for a while, then slide back into their idolatrous ways. Another nation would conquer and oppress them, they'd repent, turn back to God, and cry out for deliverance. Again and again the cycle continued.

Let's pick up the narrative in Judges 10:11–16:

> The LORD replied, "When the Egyptians, the Amorites, the Ammonites, the Philistines, the Sidonians, the Amalekites and the Maonites oppressed you and you cried to me for help, did I not save you from their hands? [God's mercy and patience]
>
> "But you have forsaken me and served other gods, so I will no longer save you. Go and cry out to the gods you have chosen. Let them save you when you are in trouble!" [Israel's faithlessness]
>
> But the Israelites said to the LORD, "We have sinned. Do with us whatever you think best, but please rescue us now." Then they got rid of the foreign gods among them and served the LORD. And he could bear Israel's misery no longer.

Did you catch that? "And he could bear Israel's misery no longer."

Does this sound like a cold, heartless, vindictive God who enjoys punishing His disobedient children? No! A thousand times, no. Like a parent who loves his children—who wants to give them everything good and spare them everything bad—His heart broke for His rebellious offspring. Again and again He pleaded for them to turn back. He forgave them, rescued them, and welcomed them back into His good favor.

In return, they trampled His mercy and kindness by again chasing every false god that promised something new and enticing. They chose the pleasure of sin for a season instead of a lifetime of God's blessing and favor.

Because He was God, He knew when Israel had reached a point where they would never return to Him again. When they turned their backs on Him for the last time, He removed His hand of protection and allowed them to be destroyed.* All the while, His heart was breaking.

At first glance, the God of the Old Testament may appear to be a God of cold-hearted wrath. But look closer, and you'll find hundreds of verses that display His heart of love.

Uncommon Thought

Like a tenderhearted parent who wants the best for his children, God's heart breaks when we rebel. He never delights in punishing those who reject His ways.

---

* While God allowed the ten tribes of the nation of Israel to be destroyed, two tribes, Judah and Benjamin, along with many of the Levites, were spared. As He promised Abraham, He continued to preserve a remnant of His people, through which the Messiah came. Jesus's Jewish genealogy is given to us in Matthew 1.

Unusual Faith

Whenever you read a passage in the Old Testament about God's judgment, look for the accompanying verses that testify of God's love. Underline them. Ask the Holy Spirit to show you God's heart for His people. Imagine how He feels when He has to discipline one of His children for disobedience when He'd rather bless them for their obedience. When you feel that God has abandoned you or is allowing you to be oppressed, look around you for evidences of His love and care.

Read Judges 10:11–16.

Honor My Miserable Mother-in-Law?

For your daughter-in-law, who loves you
. . . is better to you than seven sons.

RUTH 4:15

Mother-in-law.

Do your lips curl up in a pleasant smile when you say the word? Does your heart warm when you think of your husband's mother? Or would you describe the feeling as more like heartburn? Is your mother-in-law a friend? An enemy? Someone you merely tolerate? If I asked you to describe your MIL, would you use words like *fun*, *wise*, and *helpful*, or *bossy*, *nosey*, and *interfering*?

Regardless of whether your mother-in-law is a peach or a prune, Scripture has quite a bit to say about the other woman in your husband's life. Some of it is contained in the Old Testament book of Ruth.

In many ways, Ruth lived every woman's nightmare. But her life didn't start out that way. Falling in love with a foreigner whose family had fled to her country because of a famine, Ruth married into a very Jewish family. We can surmise from what we read in the book of Ruth that she was welcomed into her new family and taught the ways of the Lord. Then tragedy struck.

Elimelek, the patriarch of the family, died. Widowed, with no one to support her, Naomi became dependent on her sons and daughters-in-law—until both of her sons died. Naomi, whose name meant "pleasantness," called herself by a new name that reflected her emotions: *Mara*, meaning "bitter."

Strap on Ruth's sandals for a moment. Your young husband is dead. You have no children and no means of support. All you have left is your heartbroken, bitter mother-in-law.

And your faith.

Ultimately Ruth's faith delivered her. She charted a new course for her life, providing us with a powerful example to follow as we seek to live in right relationship with our own mothers-in-law. Let's sit at her feet and learn.

Ruth honored her mother-in-law. I'm confident that the two women didn't agree on everything, and maybe their personalities clashed at times. However, Ruth recognized God had placed them together. She honored Naomi as the mother of her husband, the one who had carried, birthed, and reared him to become the man she would one day marry.

Ruth loved her mother-in-law (Ruth 4:15). So much so that when Naomi decided to return to her homeland, Ruth chose to go with her. She vowed to do whatever it took to provide for both of them, acknowledging without resentment her MIL's frailty and special needs.

Ruth listened to her mother-in-law (2:2, 3:5). Although she was a grown woman, she asked for Naomi's blessing on her plan to look for work. Unfamiliar with the culture and customs, Ruth sought Naomi's counsel. God used Naomi's insight to help Ruth avoid youthful or ignorant mistakes that could have jeopardized her future or endangered her well-being.

Ruth served her mother-in-law (2:7, 17–18). She worked hard, without resentment; sacrificially, she shared her meals and never made Naomi feel as though she were a burden.

God places a high priority on the way we relate to our parents. I believe this includes our in-laws—no matter what they're like. Although, as adults, we're no longer called to obey our parents, the fifth commandment assures us that if we honor our fathers and mothers, we'll enjoy a long and fulfilling life (Deuteronomy 5:16). The book of Ruth is a beautiful example of how honoring our mothers-in-law paves the way for God to bless us.

If you're familiar with the story of Ruth, you know that as she was laboring to provide for herself and her mother-in-law, she caught the attention of a wealthy landowner.

"Why have I found such favor in your eyes that you notice me—a foreigner?" Ruth asked him.

"Boaz replied, 'I've been told all about *what you have done for your mother-in-law* since the death of your husband—how you left your father and mother and your homeland and came to live with a people you did not know before. May the LORD repay you for what you have done. May you be richly rewarded by the LORD, the God of Israel, under whose wings you have come to take refuge'" (Ruth 2:10–12, emphasis mine). Boaz recognized that Ruth's love and care for her mother-in-law was an expression of her faith in God.

Ruth married Boaz and took her place in the royal line of Christ. Naomi's no-longer-bitter heart overflowed with the joy of caring for her grandson, Obed.

The greatest treasure, though, is found in the final chapter of the book of Ruth. As the women of the town rejoiced with Naomi at the birth of her grandson, they paid Ruth a high compliment, describing her as "your daughter-in-law, who loves you and who is better to you than seven sons" (Ruth 4:15).

Uncommon Thought

Ruth's ministry to her grieving, bitter mother-in-law became a channel for God's blessings to flow into both their lives.

Unusual Faith

Take a few minutes to think about your relationship with your mother-in-law. If you're not married, think about your relationship with your mother. Is it a channel of blessing? Consider the four ways I listed that describe how Ruth interacted with her mother-in-law. Commit to implement each of these steps. Don't be discouraged if you don't see results right away. Whether or not your MIL or mother responds positively to your efforts, believe in faith that God will reward you.

Read the book of Ruth (it's only four chapters).

Who Are You Trusting In?

Let us bring the ark of the covenant of the LORD
from Shiloh to us, that when it comes among us
it may save us from the hand of our enemies.

1 SAMUEL 4:3 (NKJV)

There's nothing like a crisis to reveal a person's heart.

Our family's first financial crisis proved it. My husband and I had been married for almost four years. We were ready to begin our family, but lacked the money necessary to bring a little one into the world. So we did what any financially responsible couple (without a lot of money) did. We saved to cover medical costs and lost income while I was out on maternity leave. I worked extra days, and we cut back wherever we could.

Finally, the day came when we had met our savings goal. Now, with a nicely padded bank account, we could turn our attention to getting pregnant.

God was gracious to us, and before long, we were expecting. A month into my pregnancy, however, the engine in our car blew up. It took half our baby savings to fix it. Two weeks later, the transmission went out. Fixing it took the other half of our savings. In two months we went from nicely-padded to dead broke. We panicked.

"What are we going to do?" I wailed. "I can't work extra anymore.

We can't save that much money in only a few months. How will we pay our bills when I'm home on maternity leave?"

That's when we realized how misplaced our trust had become.

First Samuel 4 tells a similar story. The Israelites were preparing to go to war against their archenemy, the Philistines. They were a formidable foe—remember how the shepherd boy David faced off against their nine-foot-tall warrior Goliath?

The Philistines had routed them once, but the Israelites weren't afraid to face them again. They had a secret weapon—the ark of the covenant. This golden box contained artifacts from Israel's God. From the time they'd left Egypt, it had also been the place where God's presence dwelled among them. But as their love and respect for God had diminished, they'd begun to treat it like a lucky rabbit's foot. No one could vanquish them as long as they carried their talisman into battle.

"Let us bring the ark of the covenant of the LORD from Shiloh to us, that when it comes among us it may save us from the hand of our enemies" (1 Samuel 4:3 NKJV).

Did you catch their faulty thinking? "Let us bring the ark . . . that when *it* comes among us *it* may save us from the hand of our enemies."

Although they claimed to serve the almighty, all-powerful God of the universe, instead of calling on Him to be their defender and protector, they placed their trust in a golden box.

When our financial house crashed around us in the early days of my pregnancy, we realized we'd misplaced our trust for provision and protection. Instead of believing God could provide for a baby if He chose to give us one, we trusted our bank account and our ability to earn and save.

After the Philistines soundly defeated the Israelites again, Israel repented of their misplaced faith. They once again sought God's power and protection.

We repented too.

Were we wrong to set financial goals, work hard, spend carefully, and save wisely? Absolutely not. God calls Christians to be shrewd financial managers. We got off track, though, when we trusted our bank account instead of trusting God, our ultimate provider. Like the Israelites, we suffered from a heart matter. In whom were we trusting? God or someone or something else?

When the Israelites confessed, repented, and called upon God to help them conquer the Philistines, He brought about a great victory. The prophet Samuel commemorated the event by setting up a memorial stone, saying, "Thus far the LORD has helped us" (1 Samuel 7:12).

God was faithful to us too. Despite having no savings, our precious baby girl was born right on schedule. He provided the funds to pay every doctor and hospital bill (not all at once, but we never missed a payment). Three years later He gave us another baby daughter, for whom He also provided, all the way from birth, to college, and beyond. To remind us that God is our provider, our family memorial box contains two paid-in-full hospital receipts. They serve as a powerful testimony that, "thus far the LORD has helped us."

Uncommon Thought
We're often guilty of placing our trust in the provision rather than the provider himself.

Unusual Faith
Examine your life. In what areas do you find yourself worrying? Since we needn't worry when we're fully trusting in God, are you

trusting in something other than Him? Are there any areas in which you trust something other than God to meet your needs? Confess, repent, and surrender those areas to God. Then watch Him work on your behalf.

Read 1 Samuel 4:1–22.

God Hears You

In my distress I called to the
LORD; I called out to my God.
From his temple he heard
my voice; my cry came to his ears.

2 SAMUEL 22:7

The cries that awaken a mother in the middle of the night are many and varied.

There's the cry that says, I'm feeling a little lonely; it would be nice to see your face. Another cry says, Something disturbed me. I don't like it, and I think you ought to know about it. My diaper's wet or my tummy's hungry.

And then there's the cry that jerks you upright and on your feet even before your eyes are open.

A weekend with my granddaughter, Lauren, allowed me to experience all three of these cries. I was visiting and offered to babysit so my daughter and son-in-law could have an evening out.

Following their usual bedtime ritual, I bathed Lauren, read her a bedtime story, and tucked her into bed. An hour or so later, I heard her whimper. Tiptoeing to her room, I peeked in to check on her. She had lost her pacifier and was rustling around in search of it. I watched her find it in the semi-darkness, slide it into her mouth, and drift off to sleep again.

Later that night, after I had gone to bed, I again heard a cry from her room. I tiptoed to the door to check on her. Although her cries were louder than before, she settled down in a few minutes with no intervention from me.

At 5 a.m., however, it was a different story. Shrill screams pierced the air, causing me to sit straight up in bed. My daughter, now home and asleep, responded instantly, but it took several minutes before Lauren's cries subsided.

Wise parents learn to distinguish between the cries that warrant immediate attention, the ones that need monitoring, and those that are best ignored.

But regardless of the reason, mothers (and grandmothers) hear every cry. Their ears are attuned to the sound of their babies' voices, and their hearts are knit together.

God the Father is the same way. David describes His responsiveness in 2 Samuel 22:7: "In my distress I called to the LORD; I called out to my God. From his temple he heard my voice; my cry came to his ears."

God also responds to our cries for help. Psalm 91:14 reads, "'Because he loves me,' says the LORD, 'I will rescue him; I will protect him, for he acknowledges my name.'"

At times, however, in his infinite wisdom, God chooses not to respond to our requests immediately. Perhaps He knows we need to learn lessons or develop skills. Maybe He knows our faith muscles need strengthening or that waiting for His response will help develop our character. He knows that persevering in faith, even when we can't see God at work, makes us stronger.

Uncommon Thought

If you're crying out today, be comforted and encouraged by the knowledge that God hears every cry and always responds in a timely manner in the way that is best—because He loves you.

Unusual Faith

Has there been a time when God seemed deaf to your cries, but later you saw how He was working on your behalf? You can trust God for the present situation based on His faithfulness in the past. Cry out to Him, tell Him your needs, and watch to see how He responds.

Read 2 Samuel 22:1–20.

Spiritual Sandpaper

The king of Israel answered Jehoshaphat, "There
is still one prophet through whom we can inquire
of the LORD, but I hate him because he never
prophesies anything good about me, but always bad."

1 KINGS 22:8

I love a heartwarming story as much as the next person. Facebook
abounds with happy stories about round-bellied puppies rescued
from euthanasia and placed into forever homes. Deployed service-
men and women return home to a hero's welcome and their families'
waiting arms. Anonymous philanthropists donate gobs of money to
build orphanages and schools in war-torn countries.

I love warm fuzzy Bible stories too. Who doesn't rejoice when the
father wraps his prodigal son in a welcoming embrace when he finally
finds his way home? Or cry happy tears at Revelation's pronouncement that there will be no more sickness, death, or pain when Jesus
comes to establish His eternal kingdom? We love to hear, share, and
ponder stories and sermons like these.

But sermons about sin, God's standards, and His call to live holy
lives? Not so much.

We prefer our entertainment to be uplifting and soul-stirring. Like-
wise, we expect church, Christian teaching, and Christian literature

to encourage and affirm us. We expect everything to be positive and everyone to agree with us. Every time.

This desire isn't new. Two kings had a conversation about it several millennia ago, and the Old Testament records it in the book of 1 Kings 22.

Jehoshaphat, king of Judah, and Ahab, king of Israel, were planning to go to war to take back Ramoth Gilead from the Syrians. As they planned their strategy, Jehoshaphat, the godly king, thought it might be a good idea to consult the Lord.

So Ahab summoned four hundred of the prophets on his payroll. "Shall I go to war against Ramoth Gilead, or shall I refrain?" he asked.

Careful to toe the party line, remain politically correct, and refrain from saying anything that contradicted the king (or jeopardized their cushy lifestyles), they said as one man, "Go, for the Lord will give it into the king's hand" (v. 6). I can picture King Ahab nodding and smiling that smug little smirk we get when someone agrees with us and tells us how brilliant we are.

Jehoshaphat, on the other hand, was a bit more discerning. He looked around at the kowtowing bunch of yes-men and rejected their blanket endorsement.

"Is there no longer a prophet of the LORD here whom we can inquire of?" he asked.

"The king of Israel answered Jehoshaphat, 'There is still one prophet through whom we can inquire of the LORD, but I hate him because he never prophesies anything good about me, but always bad'" (vv. 7–8). Can't you just hear the whine in Ahab's voice?

But Jehoshaphat insisted, and Micaiah was summoned before the kings. On the way, Ahab's messenger put the squeeze on Micaiah. "All the other prophets encouraged the king. You'd better do the same. For once in your life, try to say something encouraging."

But Micaiah knew he answered to God, not Ahab or his henchman. Contrary to the "suggestion," and in clear opposition to all four hundred false prophets, Micaiah spoke the word of the Lord. And it wasn't good: "The LORD has put a deceiving spirit in the mouths of all these prophets of yours. The LORD has decreed disaster for you" (v. 23).

In today's world, even in the church, we sometimes act a lot like King Ahab. We prefer our books, entertainment, and even our pastor's sermons to affirm us and support our decisions—even when they contradict God's Word. Or endanger our health, relationships, or witness. Or support a philosophy or agenda that isn't biblical.

When someone dares to speak the truth, hopefully in love, we are tempted to take offense. Sometimes we take our toys and go home. We leave a church, end a friendship, or stop supporting a ministry because they stand on the authority of Scripture, and it rubs us the wrong way. We forget (or choose to ignore) that they answer to God and are called, as best as they know how, to share the whole counsel of God, not just the warm fuzzy parts. If their words align with Scripture, perhaps God is calling us to adjust our lives, not calling them to adjust their message.

In my three decades as a Christian, I've discovered that the greatest friends I have are those who will tell me the truth, based on God's Word—even if they suspect I won't receive it well. Like Micaiah before the kings, it takes courage and commitment to stand on the authority of the Bible and share a message that contradicts culture, political correctness, or popular opinion.

Instead of being offended by these brave spokespersons, we

should thank God for them. If we truly want our lives to honor God, we must set aside our pride, consider their words, and examine our behavior. If we find ourselves in error, we should ask God to show us what to do to get back on the right path.

God sent Micaiah and his message to spare God's people from destruction at the hand of the Syrians. Who knows? Perhaps the brave souls who speak truth into our lives may be God's special messengers to warn and protect us.

Uncommon Thought

When we feel the spiritual sandpaper rubbing our souls, instead of getting offended, perhaps we should look at the situation more closely. Are the words we're hearing simply a matter of opinion, or are they based on the Bible? Are they someone's preference, or could they be coming from the Lord?

Unusual Faith

The next time you feel offended by something someone says, compare their message to the Bible. If their words agree with Scripture, consider that God might be calling you to adjust your life to align more closely to His Word. Ask Him to show you what you need to change, then take the first step of obedience.

Read 1 Kings 22:1–37.

Why God Allows What He Hates

Josiah was eight years old when he became king,
and he reigned in Jerusalem thirty-one years. . . .
He did what was right in the eyes of the LORD.

2 KINGS 22:1–2

Alcohol ruled Sarah's mom and threatened to destroy her and her family.

Her mom was unkempt, had lost most of her teeth, and looked twenty years older than she was. After her divorce, her condition grew worse. She spent most days on the couch in a drunken stupor, oblivious to the needs of her children. Although my friend Sarah tried to hide her mom's condition, she came to me in tears one day, overwhelmed by the responsibility of caring for her two younger sisters.

In addition to going to high school, Sarah worked a part-time job. I suspect she often used her wages to buy food for herself and her sisters. Every morning she made sure her sisters ate breakfast, dressed, and caught the school bus. In the evenings, she helped them with their homework. But this routine wasn't what undid her.

What finally brought Sarah to the breaking point? Her four-year-old sister's hair.

"Katie's always had long baby-fine hair," she told me in tears one day. "It has to be brushed every night or it gets all knotted up. I've been so busy with work and school that I haven't had time to brush it. Now it's snarled into this giant rat's nest, and I don't know what to do. I'm afraid her teacher's going to notice and wonder what's going on at home. I'd die if social services took them away."

With patience, persistence, and gobs of hair conditioner, we unknotted Katie's hair, but it took something much more dramatic to unknot the tangles left by their mom's alcoholism.

One day Chelsea, a mutual friend, invited Sarah to church, and she said yes. Every Sunday thereafter she'd ride to church with Chelsea's family, eat dinner with them, and go back to church again that evening. It wasn't long before Sarah surrendered her life to Christ.

She took her newfound faith seriously and applied it to every area of her life. She studied hard, cared for her sisters, and continued to work.

Sarah was one of the first people to share Christ with me. When she explained her faith, I found it intellectually interesting, but that was about it. Years later, when all the pieces fell into place and I surrendered my life to God, Sarah became a spiritual example to me.

She graduated in the top ten percent of her high school class, excelled in college, married a godly man, and raised three handsome sons (in addition to her two sisters). She succeeded in business and enjoyed serving in her church.

Sarah is proof that God can redeem, restore, and rebuild. Hezekiah's grandson Josiah was too. The Bible tells us his story in 2 Kings 22.

Hezekiah was one of the godliest kings mentioned in the Bible. One day he fell ill, and Isaiah the prophet broke the news to him that he was going to die. Hezekiah begged God to heal him, and he did. He lived fifteen more years and fathered a son named Manasseh.

Manasseh succeeded Hezekiah and became one of Judah's wickedest kings, leading the people into blasphemous and idolatrous pagan worship.

This account begs us to ask, why did God add fifteen years to Hezekiah's life if Manasseh's birth would result? He was one of the worst kings in the nation's history!

The Bible doesn't tell us why. However, Manasseh was succeeded by his son Josiah. The record of Josiah's coronation may shed some light into God's purpose. The Bible records that "Josiah was eight years old when he became king, and he reigned in Jerusalem thirty-one years. . . . He did what was right in the eyes of the LORD" (2 Kings 22:1–2). He purged the land of idolatry, led the nation in a renewed commitment to the Lord, and brought back the celebration of the Passover feast.

"Neither before nor after Josiah was there a king like him who turned to the LORD as he did—with all his heart and with all his soul and with all his strength" (2 Kings 23:25).

Pastor and author Steve Estes once told quadriplegic Joni Eareckson Tada, "Sometimes God allows what He hates to accomplish what He loves."[3]

Because God has given mankind free will, sometimes He allows alcoholic moms and evil kings. Perhaps my friend Sarah's difficult home life helped her recognize her need for God. Maybe Josiah's did too. In each circumstance, God revealed himself, invited them into a personal relationship with Him, and used them in mighty ways. He broke the chain of destruction and set them on a new course.

Uncommon Thought

While God never causes evil, we can trust Him to use it for good when we surrender our lives to Him.

Unusual Faith

What part of your life would fit the description of something God hates? Can you look back and see how God used it for good in your life or someone else's? Sometimes God allows us to glimpse how He uses tragedy and hardship, and other times it remains a mystery we won't understand until heaven. Is there something you need to trust God with, by faith, until that time?

Read 2 Kings 22:1–20.

Disaster on Your Doorstep

The ark of God remained with the family of
Obed-Edom in his house for three months, and the
LORD blessed his household and everything he had.

1 CHRONICLES 13:14

Poor Obed-Edom. There he was, minding his own business, living a quiet, obscure life out in the countryside, raising his family and tending his farm. There's no mention of him on the pages of Scripture until the day disaster landed on his doorstep.

I'm sure he was aware of the procession marching near his home. Who in Israel wasn't? After twenty years, the ark of the covenant, the symbol of God's presence, was finally returning to Jerusalem. King Saul had neglected it, but King David was about to make it right. Its return was a cause for celebration—until it wasn't.

God had previously told the Israelites how to transport the ark so that no one would touch it. The ark represented God's glory and holiness, and needed to be treated with the utmost respect. In their enthusiasm to bring the ark home, David and the leaders of Israel failed to brush up on the very clear instructions God had given for handling this sacred article—with disastrous results. A man named Uzzah touched the ark and was immediately struck dead. The parade came to a screeching halt.

After the death of Uzzah, "David was afraid of God that day and asked, 'How can I ever bring the ark of God to me?'" (1 Chronicles 13:12).

If Uzzah had mishandled the ark and was struck dead, who'd be next? Would God's wrath fall on the entire company? David decided the best thing to do was to rid himself of this frightening article as quickly as possible. He turned the procession aside and dumped it at Obed-Edom's front door.

Put yourself in Obed-Edom's place. What thoughts would be running through your head?

Wait a minute. What do you mean you're leaving the ark of the covenant with me? Didn't one guy just die because he dared to touch it? What? You're afraid to bring it to Jerusalem because something bad might happen? So you're leaving it on my front porch? What about my safety? And my family's?

Although we've probably never had a dangerous artifact delivered to our front door, we can all relate to Obed-Edom. When was the last time a circumstance or situation dropped into your life that you had no control over, didn't ask for, and had no idea what to do with? A frightening, potentially dangerous situation that could change your life forever?

Author and speaker Carol Kent was at the peak of her ministry, traveling all over the world encouraging women with her down-to-earth writing and teaching style. Then came the midnight call. "Your son has been arrested for murder." In an instant, her world went black. She tells the story in her book, *When I Lay My Isaac Down: Unshakable Faith in Unthinkable Circumstances.*

Her upstanding Naval Academy graduate son, JP, was jailed, tried, convicted, and sent to prison for life with no hope of parole. In the aftermath, Carol was left to pick up the pieces of her life and ministry. Today, part of that ministry is called Speak Up for Hope, a nonprofit organization dedicated to positively impacting inmates and their families. "God can take a situation like ours," Carol says, "and redeem it for His purposes."[4]

The same was true for Obed-Edom. He responded in faith to the unexpected and frightening challenge God had allowed into his life. He trusted that if God had permitted it, then He must have a plan for it. First Chronicles 13:14 continues the story. "The ark of God remained with the family of Obed-Edom in his house for three months, and the LORD blessed his household and everything he had."

Not only did God bless Obed-Edom for three months, if you follow him through the pages of Scripture, you'll see that God blessed him and his family for generations. First Chronicles 15:21 describes how he was selected to play the harp in the procession that safely and reverently transported the ark into Jerusalem. Later he became one of the gatekeepers for the ark.

God gave him eight sons and sixty-two descendants, whom Scripture describes as "capable men with the strength to do the work" (1 Chronicles 26:8). The last reference to Obed-Edom (2 Chronicles 25:24) describes how he fulfilled the great responsibility to care for the gold, silver, and articles of the temple—the national treasures.

Obed-Edom's story is a shining example of how we should react when unexpected circumstances land on our doorsteps. Disaster can give way to delight when we trust God with it.

Uncommon Thought
God can bring great blessings out of great tragedies if we trust God and respond in faith.

Unusual Faith

I don't know what unexpected and frightening circumstance has dropped into your life. Maybe it's a job loss or an illness. An aging parent or an unexpected pregnancy. A marital challenge or a wayward child. I encourage you, like Obed-Edom and Carol Kent, to bravely accept the circumstances God has allowed. Instead of asking why, ask, "What would you have me to do, Lord?" Then trust Him to give you the ability to fulfill it.

Read 1 Chronicles 13:1–14.

Two Choices

"We have no power to face this vast army
that is attacking us. We do not know what
to do, but our eyes are on you."

2 CHRONICLES 20:12

We love choices. From the 1970s "Have It Your Way" Burger King jingle to the more than one hundred drink options in a Coca-Cola Freestyle drink machine, we like to express our preferences and make our selections.

Having designed this characteristic of human nature, God also gives us choices. Unlike one hundred drink flavors in a drink machine, however, He makes it simple. In life, we have only two choices, and these options go way back to a story in 2 Chronicles 20.

At the time, godly king Jehoshaphat sat on the throne of Judah. As is often the case with godly rulers, before long, enemies arrived to try to mess up his good thing. Judah was a shadow of her former self in those days, with an army no one in his right mind would boast about. When the big guys came knocking, King Jehoshaphat knew they were in trouble.

"A vast army is coming against you," the warning stated. Jehoshaphat was "alarmed" (2 Chronicles 20:2–3). He gathered the leaders from the surrounding cities, and together they sought the Lord.

"We have no power to face this vast army that is attacking us," he prayed. "We do not know what to do, but our eyes are on you" (v. 12).

Almost immediately, God responded to Jehoshaphat's prayer through one of the prophets. "Do not be afraid or discouraged because of this vast army. For the battle is not yours, but God's. . . . You will not have to fight this battle. Take up your positions; stand firm and see the deliverance the LORD will give you. . . . The LORD will be with you" (vv. 15, 17).

With these words, God gave Jehoshaphat two choices: believe the impossibility of the circumstances or believe God's Word. We face the same decision every day.

Picture the rest of the story. "Jehoshaphat bowed down with his face to the ground, and all the people of Judah and Jerusalem fell down in worship before the LORD" (v. 18). The next morning, per God's instructions, they marched out to face the enemy with music on their lips and praise in their mouths. "Give thanks to the LORD," they sang, "for his love endures forever" (v. 21).

Without lifting a spear or a sword, the Israelites won a great victory. The Lord fought for them. By praying, seeking God's face, and believing His promises, they released the power available in heaven. God brought it to earth for a great victory.

The result? "The fear of God came on all the surrounding kingdoms when they heard how the LORD had fought against the enemies of Israel" (v. 29).

Uncommon Thought
When faced with challenging (and sometimes overwhelming) circumstances, we can either believe what we see with our eyes or trust the promises God has given us.

Unusual Faith

What enemy are you facing right now? What circumstance steals the sleep from your night and the peace from your days? You have two choices: believe the seeming impossibility of the circumstances or believe God's promises. If you choose to believe God's promises, pray to the Lord right now. Like King Jehoshaphat, lay your circumstances before Him, confess your fear and powerlessness, and wait for His direction and deliverance.

Read 2 Chronicles 20:1–22.

The Lord Moved the Heart

In the first year of Cyrus king of Persia, in order to
fulfill the word of the LORD spoken by Jeremiah, the
LORD moved the heart of Cyrus king of Persia.

EZRA 1:1

Some days it seems like the good guys are losing—badly. News sources abound with stories about attacks on religious freedom, the erosion of the family, and crimes so heinous they require viewer warnings. Headlines proclaim, "The Church Is Dead!" and we suspect it might be true. Sunday is just another day. Our culture cries for tolerance, yet grows increasingly intolerant toward men and women of faith. Ministers fall from grace, and no one seems surprised.

When I grow discouraged and feel like God is absent—or worse, vanquished from this world—the Bible renews my hope. It reminds me that, since the dawn of time, God's plan has continued to unfold according to His will. Nothing can delay, derail, or thwart His purposes.

We find it hard to see God's governing hand in the midst of out-of-control circumstances. We so easily lose sight of the truth of God's Word. I recently discovered a short phrase in the ten-chapter book of Ezra that contained all the hope we need to restore our faith and trust.

But first, some background on the book of Ezra. You may remember that by the time of the prophets, the nation of Israel had turned away from God. Even though He had poured out His blessings and protection on them, they turned their backs on Him. They chose instead to follow the siren song of the surrounding nations. Israel disobeyed His laws, ignored His messengers, and embraced wicked, pagan practices.

Yet God was long-suffering. He called to them, begging them to repent and turn back. Finally, He pronounced judgment upon the nation through the prophet Jeremiah. "'I will summon all the peoples of the north and my servant Nebuchadnezzar king of Babylon,' declares the LORD, 'and I will bring them against this land and its inhabitants and against all the surrounding nations. I will completely destroy them and make them an object of horror and scorn, and an everlasting ruin. I will banish from them the sounds of joy and gladness, the voices of bride and bridegroom, the sound of millstones and the light of the lamp. This whole country will become a desolate wasteland, and these nations will serve the king of Babylon seventy years'" (Jeremiah 25:9–11).

When the Israelites still refused to repent, God did what He promised. He allowed the Babylonian army to destroy the temple and carry the people into exile.

Yet in Ezra 1:1, we read a phrase that reminds us how even when the world seemed to be collapsing, God's plan marched on. He was firmly, sovereignly in control.

"In the first year of Cyrus king of Persia, in order to fulfill the word of the LORD spoken by Jeremiah, *the Lord moved the heart* of Cyrus king of Persia" to rebuild the temple (Ezra 1:1, emphasis mine).

Imagine that. The Lord moved the heart of a pagan king. This godless king decided, all of a sudden—and, coincidentally, exactly seventy years after the Israelites went into exile—to rebuild the temple of a God he didn't believe in? Why? Because "the LORD moved [his] heart."

But it gets better. The king summoned all the Jews and gave them permission to return to Israel. And he offered to finance their relocation and the building project. *What?!*

And then it really gets good. Not only did God work in King Cyrus's heart, He also worked in the hearts of the Israelites. (Remember those wicked, rebellious, disobedient people who didn't want to have anything to do with God?) "Then the family heads of Judah and Benjamin, and the priests and Levites—*everyone whose heart God had moved*—prepared to go up and build the house of the LORD in Jerusalem" (Ezra 1:5, emphasis mine).

This little phrase, "everyone whose heart God had moved," reminds us of some important facts.

God has a plan for this world, and He will see it through to the end. It's a good plan, one in which evil is vanquished, and all is made right again.

God is able to move the hardest hearts and motivate anyone to do His will. No one is outside the reach of His patient and powerful arm.

We, His people, play an important part in His plan. Although He's omnipotent and could do it all himself, He's chosen to use us, frail and flawed, to be His hands and feet.

God fulfilled Jeremiah's prophecy—to the day—by stirring the heart of King Cyrus to rebuild the temple, release the exiles, and bankroll the project. Then He moved in the Israelites' hearts, causing them to want to be part of the work He was bringing about.

There are 1,239 prophecies in the Old Testament and 578 in the New Testament, for a total of 1,817 prophecies in the Bible.[5] Many have already been fulfilled. Christ alone fulfilled more than 300.

But many more remain—prophecies of Christ's second coming, end times events, the salvation of Israel, the new heaven and the new earth, the judgment of Satan, and the ushering in of God's heavenly kingdom, to name a few. Verses like the ones in Ezra remind us that God has a plan, and nothing—and no one—will stand in His way.

That's powerful comfort, don't you think?

Uncommon Thought

No matter how hell-bent our world seems, God continues to work out His plan in heaven and on earth.

Unusual Faith

If you could grasp—really grasp—the truth that nothing and no one can hinder God's good plan from moving forward, how would this affect your anxiety level? Your tendency toward fear? The way you view the events of your life? How would you live your life differently? Take a few minutes to acknowledge in prayer God's faithfulness to you. Then commit your future to Him, trusting that He will fulfill His purpose in and through your life. No matter whose heart He has to move, He will accomplish His will.

Read Ezra 1:1–11.

The Balance between All God and All Me

"We prayed to our God and posted a guard
day and night to meet this threat."

NEHEMIAH 4:9

The balance between faith and action is a delicate one. Do we install a security system or trust God to keep our family safe? Visit a doctor or pray for healing? Buy long-term-care insurance or hope that Christ returns before we grow old and frail?

Every day we face decisions that force us to choose between trusting God and trusting ourselves, but are the answers really as polarizing as they seem?

Nehemiah wrestled with this question more than two thousand years ago, and his example provides timely guidance for our twenty-first-century quandaries. While his dilemma didn't involve security systems and long-term care, it did cause him to puzzle through the balance between faith and work, God's care and human responsibility.

Although Nehemiah enjoyed a comfortable position as cupbearer to the king in the capital city of Shushan, his heart rested with his brothers in Jerusalem. Decades earlier, invading forces had ransacked the city, rounded up the majority of its citizens, and deported them. After the prophesied seventy years of captivity, a remnant had been allowed to return. When a representative from his kinfolk living in the city brought Nehemiah a heartbreaking report, he knew he had to act.

"Those who survived the exile and are back in the province are in great trouble and disgrace," the man said. "The wall of Jerusalem is broken down, and its gates have been burned with fire" (Nehemiah 1:3).

With the king's blessings, Nehemiah returned to Jerusalem to organize the citizens to rebuild the wall, the city's main defense. The project moved along nicely . . . until enemies of the Jews hatched an evil plot to ambush the workers and derail the work.

In God's providence, Nehemiah caught wind of the diabolical plan. He had a choice to make—trust God to protect them or take steps to defend themselves. Faith told him, if God has called you to this task, then He will protect you. Fear told him, the enemy is strong. How can you know for sure God will take care of you? Frightened citizens pressured him for an answer. Ten times they came to him, saying, "Wherever you turn, they will attack us" (Nehemiah 4:12).

But Nehemiah knew two things: God had called them to the work, and God would help them see it through to completion. His answer to the dilemma the Israelites faced helps us know what to do when we're stuck between God's calling and the world's opposition.

"We prayed to our God and posted a guard day and night to meet this threat" (v. 9).

Nehemiah demonstrated that we must take whatever sensible steps God shows us to address the needs of the moment, but ultimately, we must trust God to care for us.

No security system, insurance policy, or bank account can provide ultimate protection. Only God can. Yet He often uses man-made systems to meet our needs.

The person who fails to save, spends every dollar she earns, and makes no financial plan for the future is presumptuous to think God will take care of her despite her lack of foresight. The person who eschews medical care ignores the fact that God uses doctors and pharmaceuticals to heal. The person who takes foolish risks and unnecessarily endangers his health and safety, saying that he can't die until God allows it, ignores the biblical admonition not to test the Lord our God.

By the same token, those who neglect charitable giving and wise spending in order to save every dollar they make, purchase every insurance policy known to man, and avoid anything risky live as if everything depends on them. They leave no place in the equation for God.

Nehemiah found the balance. He sought God's counsel, acted wisely, and, ultimately, trusted God for the future.

We see him apply this approach throughout the book of Nehemiah. He instructed each man building the wall to carry his tool in one hand and his sword in the other. He enacted a plan to sound the alarm should danger approach, yet didn't stop the work God had called them to do.

"Don't be afraid of them," he said to the people. "Remember the Lord, who is great and awesome, and fight for your families, your sons and your daughters, your wives and your homes" (v. 14).

Work and pray. Act and trust. Labor and rest.

So often our lives swing on the pendulum between faith and action. A healthy measure of both, as Nehemiah demonstrated, is the center of God's will for us.

Uncommon Thought

Only when we bring our fears and concerns to the Lord, seek His wisdom, and respond in faith can we rest in the healthy balance between human responsibility and divine care.

Unusual Faith

Think about how you usually make decisions. Do you lean more toward faith or fear, human responsibility or God's provision? Invite God to show you if you lean too hard in one direction or the other. Ask Him if you need to correct decisions made in fear or take more responsibility in areas in which you've left Him out. The next time you have a choice to make, commit to seek God's will for the biblical balance between doing your part and trusting God to do His.

Read Nehemiah 4:1–23.

Raising the Next Generation

Every day he walked back and forth near
the courtyard of the harem to find out how
Esther was and what was happening to her.

Esther 2:11

How often do you watch a movie or TV sitcom where the parent is the hero? Never? Almost never? In today's child-centered age, children and adolescents shine in the spotlight, and parents either play a minor role or act like idiots.

On the surface, this scenario is also true of the Old Testament book of Esther. But if you read the story with a director's eye, you'll discover that Esther's heroism is made possible, in large part, by one of the book's often-overlooked supporting characters, Mordecai.

Like Cinderella, the story of Esther contains all the components of a box office hit. A handsome king, a beautiful queen, an evil villain, and an epic battle. Its plots, subplots, twists, turns, humor, and a surprise ending keep you reading till the last satisfying chapter. My favorite part is the Oscar-winning performance by Esther's adopted father.

If we study this little book closely, we'll find five qualities we can emulate as we seek to rear our children or inspire others to be heroes and heroines in God's kingdom.

Scripture doesn't tell us about the tragedy that separated Esther from her parents. All we know is that Mordecai took her in "as his own daughter when her father and mother died" (Esther 2:7).

Along with other young maidens, Esther was ripped away from Mordecai and conscripted to the harem that served King Xerxes. Esther found favor with the king and eventually became his queen. If this were a Disney movie, the curtain would close on the fairy tale ending, but this story contains much more.

Like Esther, Mordecai was a faithful Jew who loved God. Unfortunately, his devotion created an enemy—the evil Haman. Angered by Mordecai's commitment to bow his knee only to God, Haman hatched an evil plot to destroy him and his Jewish countrymen.

Only Esther could save them by approaching the king and begging for their lives. With courage and faith, she enacted a bold and creative plan, but her success rested firmly on the foundation of her upbringing as the adopted daughter of Mordecai.

Whether we're parenting children of our own or simply trying to set a godly example for others to follow, we can learn from Mordecai. Let's take a look at his actions, how they impacted Esther's story, and how we might follow his example today.

He acted courageously. Mordecai distinguished himself when he uncovered and reported a plot to kill King Xerxes (Esther 2:21–22). Courage, like many other virtues, is learned best when modeled. We can be sure Mordecai's brave example made an impression on his young charge.

He did what was right, even when it cost him something. When the king's edict dictated that all bow before Prime Minister Haman, Mordecai remained standing. To kneel would have been an act of idolatry. His bold refusal put him squarely in Haman's crosshairs (Esther 3:1–6).

In a world that's becoming increasingly hostile to the truth of God's Word, we, too, must sometimes take unpopular stands when society, culture, or even law requires us to do something contrary to what the Bible says.

He continued to watch and pray over Esther, even though his "official" responsibility of raising her was over. Many have a false belief that parenting ends when a child goes off to college. Mordecai's example shows us we should always keep watch, albeit mostly from a distance. "Every day he walked back and forth near the courtyard of the harem to find out how Esther was and what was happening to her" (Esther 2:11).

As my younger daughter prepared to attend college, I gathered a group of friends with young adult children to meet monthly to pray for our kids. Almost a decade later, we're still meeting. We've prayed our children through exams, graduation, relationships, marriages, and careers. Now some of us are praying for our grandchildren. Regular prayer is a powerful way to keep spiritual watch over those we love.

He challenged Esther to stay true to her people and her faith, even if it meant endangering her life. Mordecai reminded Esther that she was, first and foremost, a Jew—one of God's chosen people. No royal title, expatriot status, or social dictate changed that. "Do not think that because you are in the king's house you alone of all the Jews will escape," Mordecai told her (Esther 4:13).

The privilege of being God's children comes with the responsibility to speak up and defend God's Word, His principles, and His people. This was true in Esther's day, and it remains true today. Like Mordecai, we must remind our children of this responsibility when they face the temptation to blend into the crowd instead of standing with God's people and doing what is right.

He trusted God's sovereignty, but also recognized that God uses people to accomplish His will. Because Mordecai had studied Scripture, he knew God would preserve the Jewish nation. He also knew God typically raised up deliverers from among His people. By challenging Esther to speak up on behalf of her countrymen, he invited her to take her place among the champions of the faith. "For if you remain silent at this time," Mordecai said, "relief and deliverance for the Jews will arise from another place, but you and your father's family will perish. And who knows but that you have come to your royal position for such a time as this?" (Esther 4:14).

We can't presume to know how God will act in others' lives, but we can remind them of the truths of Scripture and encourage them to step out in faith. By doing so, they may even discover their destiny.

Those familiar with the story of Esther know God brought great deliverance to the Jews through her courageous acts. Because of her stand, she became a heroine of the faith. I'm convinced that Esther wouldn't have succeeded without Mordecai's godly counsel.

Uncommon Thought
As Christian parents, grandparents, and mentors, perhaps God has called us to raise the next generation of faith-filled defenders, "for such a time as this."

Unusual Faith
We're all called to lead by example as Mordecai did, making disciples and raising up the next generation. Who are the physical or spiritual children in your circle of influence who could benefit from your insight and experience? If there are none, why not? Ask God to give you eyes to see who around you needs a mentor. When you find them, prayerfully explore the next step together.

Read Esther 2:1–17.

What Is God Doing?

These are but the outer fringe of his works; how
faint the whisper we hear of him! Who then
can understand the thunder of his power?

JOB 26:14

Do you ever wonder what in the world God is doing in your crazy, frustrating life?

What good does it do to keep reaching out to difficult people when they don't seem to care? Why is that ministry thriving and yours just limping along? Why did you spend half your life teaching your kids to love God only to have them turn their backs on faith? Why should you keep praying when nothing ever changes? If you're obeying God's call, why is it so hard?

God, what are you doing in this crazy life of mine?

If you can relate to any of these questions, there's hope. Hope that comes, of all places, from the book of Job.

Who would think a man who had lost ten children in a tragic accident, went from millionaire to pauper in a day, and was married to a cruel, faithless woman would have any hope to offer? But in God's upside-down economy, it's not surprising at all.

In the twenty-sixth chapter, Job reminds his "miserable comforters" of the might, power, and majesty of God.

"He suspends the earth over nothing," Job says. "He wraps up the waters in his clouds. . . . By his power he churned up the sea. . . . By his breath the skies became fair" (Job 26:7–13).

Then he concludes with this awe-struck realization: "And these are but the outer fringe of his works; how faint the whisper we hear of him! Who then can understand the thunder of his power?" (Job 26:14).

The outer fringe of His works.

I grew up on the rocky shores of Narragansett Bay in Bristol, Rhode Island. I'd often sit at the shoreline, wade in the shallows, or swim out until my feet barely touched the bottom. Because I had lived around the sea all my life, I thought I knew it well.

Then one day I boarded a ship that took me hundreds of miles offshore, where the water stretched from horizon to horizon and the ocean floor lay miles beneath me. Only then did I begin to understand the vast nature of the ocean. Before that, I had experienced only the outer fringe—and how faint a whisper it had been.

After pointing out our nearsighted perspective, Job lifts the fog on the ocean of God's ways: "Who then can understand the thunder of his power?"

In 1 Corinthians, Paul writes: "What no eye has seen, what no ear has heard, and what no human mind has conceived—the things God has prepared for those who love him" (2:9). And, "Now we see only a reflection as in a mirror" (13:12).

As Christians temporarily tethered to the earth by our mortality, we glimpse only the outer fringe of His works. And hear only small whispers of Him.

But one day we'll sail out into the vast expanse of no-time life. We'll hear the clarion call of God's mighty voice. We'll witness the thunder of His power. And we will understand.

Every Bible verse you taught your children? Seed for the harvest.

Every hour spent responding patiently to difficult people? Sandpaper smoothing the edges of your soul.

Every late night and early morning prayer time? A fragrant offering.

Every kind deed done in Jesus's name? Stepping stones on the journey toward godliness.

Job can speak into our angst and impatience because he, too, wondered what in the world God was doing. How could anything good be happening when he saw so few results?

But Job clung to his integrity, remained faithful to God, and never stopped believing that somehow, somewhere, God was using his suffering to bring about a mighty harvest.

"I know that my redeemer lives," he declared triumphantly, "and that in the end he will stand on the earth. And after my skin has been destroyed, yet in my flesh *I will see God*" (Job 19:25–26, emphasis mine).

Because of the gift of Scripture, we know what Job didn't—that God was using the panorama of his life, the pain and the pleasure, to write a faith story so genuine that it would encourage believers for millennia.

We know none of Job's heart-wrenching experiences were wasted. Even today, thousands of years later, God continues to use his insight and example to encourage us along our journey.

Perhaps God is using our lives to do the same for others.

The writer of Hebrews promises, "God is not unjust; he will not forget your work and the love you have shown him as you have helped his people and continue to help them" (6:10).

Today, if you're wondering what in the world God is doing in your crazy, frustrating life, be encouraged. These are only the outer fringe of His works. The vast ocean of God's good plan lies before you.

Uncommon Thought

As Christians bound to the earth by our mortality, we don't see the whole picture of what God is doing. What we are seeing is only a glimpse of the edges, only a whisper of the thunder of His power.

Unusual Faith

Sometimes we can look back at times in our lives and see how God used our hardships and trials to accomplish something amazing. Other times the curtain remains closed. When you think about Job and others from Bible history (Moses, Joseph, David, the widow from Elijah's day, Naomi, Hannah), do you think they knew fully how God was going to use their difficulties for His glory?

It's safe to assume, then, since the same God who ordered the events of their lives also orders ours, He is similarly at work in our lives. Although it's hard to conceive how anything good could come out of a dark time, imagine how God might use your struggles to bring about something amazing. If what we see is only the outer fringe of His works, what might the whole ocean look like? Ponder this question.

Read Job 26:7–14.

When Hope Is Gone

I would have lost heart, unless I had
believed that I would see the goodness
of the LORD in the land of the living.

PSALM 27:13 (NKJV)

When I was seventeen years old, a classmate tried to commit suicide. She was a star athlete with good grades and a steady boyfriend. Jill had no obvious reason to end her life. Mercifully, she didn't succeed. She later told her therapist that she had pointed the gun to her head and pulled the trigger because she had lost hope.

"'Hope' is the thing with feathers / That perches in the soul / And sings the tune without the words / And never stops—at all—," Emily Dickinson wrote, but for my friend, hope did stop, at least for a time.

Twenty years of scientific research conducted by positive psychology founder Martin Seligman revealed that hope reduces feelings of helplessness, boosts happiness, reduces stress, and improves our quality of life.[6] We cannot live long without hope.

But what is hope?

For much of the world, hope is nothing more than a wish. "I hope I get that promotion," or "I hope things will get better." It has no foundation or object. When the winds of circumstance change, hope goes with it.

For believers, hope is so much more. It's inexorably linked to our trust in God. Several Hebrew words for *trust* may even be translated "to hope" in English. Jeremiah used one of these words when he said to God, "Our hope is in you" (Jeremiah 14:22).

Hope is tightly knitted to the future. BibleStudyTools.org's dictionary entry on hope links the two. "Where suffering is present, the term may indicate that the individual is bearing affliction patiently while hopefully waiting for the Lord's deliverance."[7]

Hope is the ability to see possible good in future events, even when the events are potentially negative. Holocaust survivor Viktor Frankl clung to hope by imagining how he could one day use his nightmare experience in a concentration camp to help others cope with their own trials and tragedies.

Christians, then, don't cling to a wispy thread of wishes. Instead, we base our hope for the future on God's faithfulness in the past. We stake our trust on God's character and faithfulness.

The Psalmist who penned Psalm 27 articulated this thought when he said, "I would have lost heart, unless I had believed that I would see the goodness of the LORD in the land of the living" (v. 13 NKJV).

So how do we maintain hope?

Pastor and teacher Chuck Swindoll, in his article, "Hope beyond Hurt," recommends journaling as one way to reflect on God's faithfulness. "I look back by reading through the journals that I have kept over the years. This often helps me see a consistent pattern of God's faithfulness through old trials, which gives me confidence that any new struggle I face may be just as difficult and just as temporary. As a result, I find myself enduring hurt with a lot less fear."[8]

The strategy of looking back is biblical and finds its origin in the Passover festival. On the eve of the Israelites' exodus from Egypt, God gave Moses instructions for annually commemorating how God delivered them from the bondage of slavery. Remembering God's faithfulness and mighty acts on their behalf inspired the Israelites to trust God for the future. We, too, can look back on God's faithfulness through the challenges of our lives and the lives of those who have gone before us. There we can find inspiration to trust God for the future.

Another way to remain hopeful is to meditate on and claim God's promises. But to meditate on them, we must know them. Regular Bible reading is crucial. When I struggled with despair over a wayward child, I clung to the promise God gave me one morning during my daily Bible reading, "They will be my people, and I will be their God. I will give them singleness of heart and action, so that they will always fear me and that all will then go well for them and for their children after them" (Jeremiah 32:38–39). Years later, when God's promise to me came true, I recorded it in my journal. I often refer back to it to encourage others or bolster my own faith.

I don't know if my classmate ever found the true hope that can only be found in God, but I pray she did. When we're tempted to despair, biblical hope becomes the anchor for our souls. This steadfast hope was the only reason the writer of Psalm 27 could conclude his song with this faith-filled exhortation: "Wait for the LORD; be strong and take heart and wait for the LORD" (v. 14).

Uncommon Thought
We base our hope for the future on what God has done in the past.

Unusual Faith

What circumstance or situation tempts you to give up hope? Surrender it to God today. Ask Him to give you promises to cling to and fill your heart with hope.

Read Psalm 27:1–14.

Speak Up for Those Who Can't

Speak up for those who cannot speak for themselves,
for the rights of all who are destitute. Speak up and
judge fairly; defend the rights of the poor and needy.

PROVERBS 31:8–9

I was way outside my comfort zone.

For years I've supported pro-life ministries, and I've attended the annual March for Life rally at the statehouse. I've even volunteered at crisis pregnancy centers. But when I stood praying outside the local Planned Parenthood abortion clinic, I experienced a new level of advocacy for the unborn.

You might be tempted to skip this devotion for one of several reasons. Maybe you've had an abortion, and your heart hurts every time you think about it. Maybe you know someone who has had one and understand how painful the subject is. Maybe you'd rather pretend the problem doesn't exist or wish it would just go away. Or maybe you're a pro-life warrior who's weary of championing the cause. It's been more than forty years since *Roe v. Wade*, and the country seems no closer to outlawing abortion than when the decision was handed down. Whatever your hesitation, I encourage you to stay with me.

One fall day I stood outside an abortion clinic with four other women to pray. Just pray. No shouting at patients or waving placards with gory pictures. No in-your-face confrontations. Just silent, reverent prayer for the people who would walk through the doors of Planned Parenthood.

That particular Tuesday was an abortion day. Studies have shown that the number of no-shows for abortion appointments rises to 75 percent when volunteers pray outside clinics.[9]

Bethany, a young woman in her late twenties, was also there to pray. In between our prayers, she shared her story.

"My mother and father were seventeen years old and unmarried when they found out she was pregnant. He encouraged her to have an abortion. Thinking it was their only option, she agreed. That Saturday he drove her to a clinic in the next town.

"While he sat in the waiting area," Bethany continued, "my mother lay on the steel table in the procedure room. Clothed only in a hospital gown, she waited nervously for the doctor to come in. Suddenly, a voice shouted into her heart, 'Get out! Don't stop to get dressed, just GET OUT.'

"Certain the voice was God speaking to her, she leaped off the table, gathered her clothing, and ran out into the waiting room.

"'We have to leave,' she told her shocked boyfriend. 'I can't do this.'

"They left, told their parents about the pregnancy, and chose instead to carry the baby. Six months later, she gave birth to a beautiful, dark-haired, dark-eyed baby girl.

"That baby was me," Bethany said, blinking back tears. "I have no explanation for the voice my mother heard. But I often wonder if someone was praying that day—asking God to spare unborn babies from death and help frightened women realize that abortion isn't the only option."

That day, as I looked into Bethany's tender eyes, I vowed never to stop championing the cause of the unborn.

Proverbs 31:8–9 calls the godly to "speak up for those who cannot speak for themselves, for the rights of all who are destitute. Speak up and judge fairly; defend the rights of the poor and needy."

I can't think of a needier, more helpless group of people than the millions of tiny babies who die every year in abortion clinics across the country.

We can't all give to support pro-life efforts, but some of us can. Not everyone can volunteer, or advocate, or vote, but many of us can. Not everyone is brave enough to counsel on the street corner or carry a sign. But everyone can pray.

As I learned on the street corner that day, even if only one baby is saved, it will be worth it.

Just ask Bethany.

Uncommon Thought
We may not be able to save all the babies who are threatened by abortion, but maybe, by praying, giving, volunteering, voting, and advocating, we can save some.

Unusual Faith
As you read Bethany's story, did you feel the Lord speaking to you? Take a few moments to sit quietly before Him and ask, "Lord, what would you have me to do to speak up for the unborn?" Maybe He'll call you to give to or volunteer at a crisis pregnancy center or research and vote for pro-life candidates. Or write a letter to your local newspaper,

march in a pro-life rally, or respectfully share your concerns with your congressman or woman. Maybe, right now, all you can do is pray—don't underestimate the power of prayer in God's work. Whatever He tells you to do, do it.

Read Proverbs 6:16–19.

How Do We Approach God's House?

Guard your steps when you go to the
house of God. Go near to listen.

ECCLESIASTES 5:1

My Christian life has included worship that is solemn and liturgical as well as free-spirited and unscripted. I've attended church in a cathedral with soaring ceilings and stained glass, and I've worshiped in a store-front room with folding chairs and traffic noise.

I've heard God speak in both settings. And I've felt Him strangely silent. What makes the difference? Ecclesiastes 5:1 gives us a clue.

"Guard your steps when you go to the house of God," King Solomon writes. "Go near to listen."

I don't know about you, but I often fling myself into church as carelessly as I jaunt off to the corner store. I approach it as if it were just another activity or commitment. My casual approach to church is ironic, really, because the hours I spend there could be the most life-changing hours of my week—if I prepare for them.

My formal church upbringing taught me to revere God's house. I learned to approach the sanctuary with respect. To cease frivolous chatter, pause at the threshold, and acknowledge I was in a holy place.

The solemn music set the tone for the seriousness of the hour. We arrived early enough to sit quietly in our pews and pray, preparing our hearts. The hush that pervaded the air hinted at what was to come. These practices set the tone for the meeting that was to take place between me and God. Solomon called it guarding our steps.

The less-solemn services I've been a part of have also taught me important things. In these joyful, exuberant gatherings, I've experienced whole-hearted worship, passionate Bible teaching, and transparent prayer and confession. I've heard life-changing testimonies and witnessed powerful demonstrations of corporate unity. When I set my heart and mind to listen, I hear God speak all around me. This is what Solomon described when he said, "Go near to listen."

Regardless of what denomination or style of worship we prefer, if we want to hear from God, we must heed Solomon's words and apply them. Here are several practices that have helped me:

Prepare for Sunday on Saturday night. As much as possible, do things in advance to make Sunday morning easier. Sometimes I'll put together a simple breakfast casserole or bake muffins I can pair with fruit for an easy meal. Sunday morning is not the day for elaborate breakfasts. Selecting the clothes I'll wear the next day gives me the opportunity to iron a few wrinkles or find that missing shoe.

Go to bed at a reasonable hour. It's impossible to concentrate in church on Sunday morning if I've stayed up too late on Saturday night. I wonder how many life-changing sermons or game-changing lessons I've snoozed through because I didn't prepare my mind by giving it adequate rest. I almost never stay up too late on a work night because I don't want my work to suffer. Why would I stay up too late the night before I go to God's house?

Begin Sunday morning with prayer. Even before you get out of bed, dedicate the day to God. "Lord, this is your day. Keep Satan far from it. Help me glorify you in all that I do." (This is actually an excellent prayer to pray at the start of every day, because every day is the Lord's.)

Before the service starts, quiet your heart and mind. This isn't the time to chat it up with your friends or touch base with your BFF about next week's lunch date. Close your eyes, breathe deeply, and pause. Thank God for allowing you into His presence. Pray, "Lord, give me ears to hear what you want to teach me. Make my heart tender to receive your words. Show me any sin I need to confess. Speak to me today."

Solomon's wise words remind us, "Guard your steps when you go to the house of God. Go near to listen." God will meet us there.

Uncommon Thought
We prepare for just about everything in life, but we often approach our worship experience casually.

Unusual Faith
Think about your normal approach to Sunday worship. Are you intentional or haphazard? Do you prepare in advance or just let it happen? Consider Solomon's encouragement to guard our steps and go near to listen. What might this look like in your life? Choose one suggestion from the list above or try one of your own that might help you hear from God more clearly the next time you're in church. Put at least one idea into practice this week and see what a difference it makes.

Read Ecclesiastes 5:1–7.

Keeping the Spark Alive

This is my love, and this is my friend.
SONG OF SONGS 5:16 (HCSB)

"Give me a fist bump before you go, sweetie," my husband said as I prepared to leave for a meeting. He was recovering from a stomach bug, and I was still fighting the remnants of a nasty head cold. For weeks, in an attempt not to share germs, we'd stopped kissing and resorted to fist bumps. It was a temporary trade, but, sadly, when it comes to physical intimacy, many marriages are permanently stuck at fist bumps.

Sexual attraction never looks complicated on television. A man and a woman catch each other's eye across a crowded coffee shop. He smiles. She glances down. When she looks up again, his eyes are still fixed on her. This time, she holds his gaze, lifts an eyebrow, and smiles a Mona Lisa smile. The faces of the other customers blur into the background, and the rhythm of their beating hearts drowns out everything else.

Sure, some of us have had a few television moments in our lives, but they're the exception rather than the rule. Truth be told, it's hard to keep the embers of physical intimacy smoldering in a marriage. Parenting, work, and a thousand other distractions cool the passion of the early years. "Tired bodies make for tired sex," a wise counselor once told me, and it's true. What once came naturally and spontaneously now must be intentional, approached with anticipation, planned for, and mustered up. If we're not careful, passionate kisses become fist bumps, and lovers morph into roommates.

Perhaps this is why the Lord dedicated an entire book of the Bible to the subject of marital intimacy. We read (in sometimes voyeuristic detail) the steamy exchange of compliments between Solomon and his new bride.

"How handsome you are, my beloved! Oh, how charming! And our bed is verdant. . . . His arms are rods of gold set with topaz. His body is like polished ivory decorated with lapis lazuli" (Song of Songs 1:16; 5:14).

"Your lips drop sweetness as the honeycomb, my bride; milk and honey are under your tongue" (4:11).

The sensual, playful abandon of Solomon and his love give a godly nod to the joys of intimacy and encourage couples to pursue the spark of passion in the ordinary of the everyday. And pursue it we must.

Lest your kisses become fist bumps, whether you're already married or might be at some point, here are a few suggestions for maintaining physical intimacy within your marriage:

Flirt with your husband. Take a page out of Song of Songs and tell him how soft his lips are, how much you admire his muscles, or how you love the color of his eyes.

Watch your thoughts. Intimacy for women begins in our minds and how we think about our husbands. Channeling our thoughts into positive expressions of respect and admiration toward them softens and prepares our minds as well as our bodies.

Plan, at least once a week, to go to bed early—before you're tired. That wise counselor was right, tired bodies make for tired sex. Going to bed before you're ready to go to sleep enables you to enter into romance with energy and enthusiasm.

Every now and then, step outside your comfort zone. If you usually sleep in a T-shirt, wear a nightie instead. If you don't normally use perfume or scented lotion, pamper yourself. If your husband usually initiates, surprise him by inviting him to a romantic rendezvous.

Solomon and his bride remind us that sex is a gift to be shared and enjoyed within the marriage relationship. Culture tells us it should be effortless, but experience proves even the most special gift requires effort to unwrap. When we allow our marriages to slide into physical apathy, we not only weaken them, we endanger them.

Although the book is best known as a primer for the married, tucked into its eight steamy chapters is a solemn caution for the hoping-to-be married, the almost married, and the unmarried. Three times the Shulamite warns the women of Jerusalem: "Do not stir up or awaken love until the appropriate time" (2:7; 3:5; 8:4 HCSB).

In our sex-saturated culture where "everyone" is having sex and "no one" is waiting, these verses serve as a solemn warning. Don't settle, the Shulamite says. Don't ruin something God created to be beautiful, and holy, and exclusive by rushing into a physical relationship without the commitment of marriage.

The same fire that can warm and light a home within the confines of a fireplace can burn a house down if taken outside its intended boundaries. Remaining sexually pure while single honors God, honors those we date, and honors our future spouse. The best way to prepare for the exclusivity of the marriage relationship is to remain pure outside of it. This subtle yet equally valuable message from the Song of Songs demonstrates the high esteem God places on sexual purity for all.

In Song of Songs 5:16, the Shulamite describes her husband in a way that captures the sweet, romantic possibilities of marriage. "This is my love," she says, "and this is my friend" (HCSB). Intentionally pursuing physical intimacy, means we save fist bumps for flu season and cultivate passion as a regular part of marriage.

Uncommon Thought

Song of Songs reminds us not to devalue the importance of physical intimacy. It's a unique, heavenly-designed glue that binds two people together.

Unusual Faith

Are you married? Does the romantic part of your marriage need a spark? Review the four suggestions above and choose one (or come up with one of your own). Commit to apply it to your marriage this week. But don't stop there. Make it your goal to concentrate on this important area of your marriage.

And if you're not married? Examine your thoughts and actions toward the men in your life. Commit anew to interact with them in ways that are pure and above reproach.

Read Song of Songs 1:1–17.

Pleasing the Warrior King

He tends his flock like a shepherd: He gathers the
lambs in his arms and carries them close to his
heart; he gently leads those that have young.

Isaiah 40:11

The early chapters of the book of Isaiah describe a scene that would make the most epic 3-D film look like a kindergartener's cartoon. Isaiah describes smoke, thunderous noise, and angelic multitudes crying out in praise before almighty God in His temple. A glimpse of God in His throne room fills Isaiah with awe and fear. "Woe to me!" he cries. "I am ruined!" (Isaiah 6:5).

Other Scriptures reinforce this image of God, picturing Him as the conquering King, righteous Judge, mighty Warrior, and powerful Sovereign. They describe how the oceans churn or quiet at God's command. One word from God speaks the world into existence. Another has the power to send it up in smoke. With a flick of His mighty arm, thunderbolts fly from heaven. An angry glance from His all-seeing eyes causes the earth to swallow those who disobey His commands.

"See," Isaiah 40:10 reads, "the Sovereign Lord comes with power, and he rules with a mighty arm."

No doubt about it, God is strong. And God is active.

I've always admired these attributes of God (even though I find them more than slightly terrifying), because I like strength and activity. I'm a doer, not a sitter. These character traits fit well with my assumption that God expects me to be like Him and work hard on His behalf.

But then I had children.

And my busy, do-lots-of-stuff-for-God life came to a screeching halt. Forget teaching a class, working in the bus ministry, or helping with every function the church sponsored. I could barely get myself and my baby dressed and out the door to attend worship on Sundays. Then my baby had colic (to which I wouldn't subject any nursery worker in the world). After colic, she had separation anxiety. She was three years old before she'd go into a toddler class so I could attend adult Sunday School again. Six months later, her sister was born, and I was again barely making it to church on Sundays.

My days of do-it-all ministry had come to an end. As far as the kingdom was concerned, I was useless. A taker instead of a giver. A dead weight on the gospel ship. My heart sank to think how disappointed God must be with me.

Then I read Isaiah 40:11: "He tends his flock like a shepherd: He gathers the lambs in his arms and carries them close to his heart; he gently leads those that have young."

Suddenly, I understood that the mighty Warrior is also a tender shepherd. The conquering King stoops down to lift the fragile and the frail. The righteous Judge carries His children, not as a burden on His back, but as a treasure near His heart. The powerful Sovereign gently leads those who are emotionally tender and physically sapped. Boy, did that describe me in those early childrearing years.

Through Isaiah's beautiful picture of God, I learned I didn't have to be productive for God to love me. I didn't have to perform to earn

His favor. I was free to accept what I saw as my season of "inactivity," knowing God had not only ordained it, but had a good plan for it. In His tenderness, He would carry me through my season of mothering if I would rest in Him and allow Him to lead me. Isaiah's picture of God gently leading those with young gave me permission to be frail and vulnerable, knowing that He wouldn't drive me with His rod, but would lead me with His shepherd's crook.

My children are grown now, and I'm "busy" for the Lord again. As I look back on those childrearing years, I see that they were not fruitless. Once I realized that different seasons of life bring new and different opportunities to minister, I was free to embrace each season instead of chafe at it. I learned to look for ways to be Jesus's hands and feet wherever I was, knowing that each day was ripe with potential. And I never again worried that I wasn't productive enough to satisfy Him.

Uncommon Thought
We can rest in the fact that the great I Am is not frustrated by our frailties or impatient with our humanity. Instead, He leads us like a shepherd all the way through our earthly journey.

Unusual Faith
Think a moment about your perception of God. Do you see Him as a stern taskmaster, demanding and hard to please? Or do you see Him as a shepherd, gentle and understanding toward your frailties? Do you feel as though you never measure up? That you can't do enough to please Him, especially if you're in a season of life that feels unproductive?

Spend time meditating on Isaiah 40:11. Imagine yourself as the lamb the prophet writes about. Picture yourself in the arms of the

Savior, carried close to His heart. Ask God to lead you into a greater understanding of His love and care for you. Then follow where He leads you, trusting that He will use you for His glory, no matter your season of life.

Read Isaiah 40:9–13.

JEREMIAH

Bloom with Grace

"Build houses and settle down; plant gardens and eat
what they produce. Marry and have sons and daughters;
find wives for your sons and give your daughters in
marriage, so that they too may have sons and daughters.
Increase in number there; do not decrease. Also,
seek the peace and prosperity of the city to which
I have carried you into exile. Pray to the LORD for
it, because if it prospers, you too will prosper."

JEREMIAH 29:5–7

It was hard not to notice the young woman slumped in the chair across from me. Sitting beside her mom in the reception room, she refused to make eye contact with anyone. She sat, arms crossed, sullen and silent. When her mother leaned over and gently touched her, she jerked her arm away and scowled. Without saying a word, she communicated loudly and clearly: I do *not* want to be here.

At some time or another, we've all been in this young woman's shoes. Sometimes the place we don't want to be is minor—a restaurant everyone else loves but we hate. Or at an activity our spouse enjoys but we think is boring. I've even seen this look on people's faces in church. I always wonder what prompted them to come if they so obviously didn't want to be there.

Sometimes, though, the issue is bigger than our least favorite restaurant or a movie we'd prefer not to watch. Sometimes life throws us into situations or places we'd rather not go.

Such was the case with the Jews, as told in the book of Jeremiah. For decades God had called them to forsake their worship of false gods and return to Him. He sent prophet after prophet to tell them how much He loved them and how He longed to bless them. He warned them of His coming judgment if they refused to turn from their wicked ways. But they continued blithely down the path of destruction.

And destruction came. Babylonian armies under King Nebuchadnezzar conquered and razed the city, tore down its walls, and destroyed the temple. All who remained alive after the slaughter were deported and marched off to Babylon where they lived in exile. God's people were thrown into the teeming cesspool of a pagan world.

But God, in His tenderhearted mercy, refused to forsake them. Even during their time of punishment, He was there, calling to them, reminding them of His promises, and assuring them of His love. "When seventy years are completed for Babylon," He said, "I will come to you and fulfill my good promise to bring you back to this place" (Jeremiah 29:10). But in the meantime, He instructed, this is how they should live:

> Build houses and settle down; plant gardens and eat what they
> produce. Marry and have sons and daughters; find wives for
> your sons and give your daughters in marriage, so that they too
> may have sons and daughters. Increase in number there; do not
> decrease. Also, seek the peace and prosperity of the city to which

I have carried you into exile. Pray to the LORD for it, because if it prospers, you too will prosper.

In other words, don't sit and sulk, marking time until you can leave. Instead, be fully engaged. Put down roots. Get involved. Make the place better. Even if you don't want to be there, be all there.

Most of us have never been carried off into exile, but we can relate to the Jews of Jeremiah's time. Perhaps a job loss or transfer has carried us to an unfamiliar place. Or health challenges confine us to home or a care facility. Maybe we're stuck in a situation we hope is temporary but fear will be permanent. Limited finances may limit our choices and trap us in a quagmire of despair.

God's message to the Jews is His message to us as well: be all in. Live in such a way that whatever you touch is better. Let your faith and hope shine light into the dark corners. Pray for the people around you. Infuse the air with the scent of His grace. Be hopeful, helpful, and wholehearted. When we do, not only do we positively impact the people around us, we pave the way for God to work in unexpected ways in our own lives.

Uncommon Thought

Whether you're somewhere for a day or a decade, work hard, smile often, and trust that God has you there for His good purposes.

Unusual Faith

When you find yourself in a difficult relationship, a challenging work or home situation, or a frustrating season of life, take comfort in knowing you are not outside of God's sight and care. If you doubt

God's ability to care for your needs, confess and repent of your lack of faith. Instead of merely marking time, resolve today to become fully engaged, trusting God to use your efforts for your good and His glory.

Read Jeremiah 29:1–14.

Does God Delight in Our Suffering?

For no one is cast off by the Lord forever.
Though he brings grief, he will show compassion,
so great is his unfailing love. For he does not
willingly bring affliction or grief to anyone.

LAMENTATIONS 3:31–33

I didn't know my friend from high school was dying. We hadn't seen each other in years, but when our paths crossed in the dental office, we time-warped back to our teenage years. Lena had bought me my first Chick-fil-A sandwich. And my first Helen Reddy album. Twenty-five years later, I can still sing the lyrics to the title song "I Am Woman." We'd attended church together, taken bus rides all over the city, and shared our dreams. I hoped to write the Great American Novel. She wanted to travel the country in a VW bus.

Although we lived in the same town, we drifted apart when Lena went to work and I went to college. Mutual friends would mention her occasionally, and the reports weren't good.

"She's partying a lot," one friend said.

"I see her with a different guy every time," another commented. "She's changed. You wouldn't recognize her."

They were right. The woman I bumped into in the dental office bore little resemblance to my high school friend. She sported bright pink hair. Her normally chubby cheeks were sunken, stretched tightly against her prominent cheekbones. "You look great," I lied, hugging her gently, afraid if I squeezed too hard she might break.

As we talked, our conversation turned to spiritual things.

"I've been wanting to study the Bible again," Lena said, "but I don't know where to start."

"Why don't we study together?" I said. She agreed, and we decided to meet every Tuesday night to study the book of 1 Peter.

On the first night of our study, she told me she was dying.

Her lifestyle had resulted in a fatal disease. "I felt okay at first," she said, "but I've been getting sicker. Doctors have tried several different treatments, but nothing seems to help."

When the conversation turned to spiritual things, as it often does when someone knows they're dying, I asked the question weighing heavily on my heart.

"Lena, do you know for sure, if you were to die, that you'd go to heaven?"

"Yes," she said softly, raising tear-filled eyes to meet mine. "When I was first diagnosed, I was angry at God. I knew He could have prevented me from getting sick. But then I realized that if I hadn't gotten sick, I would have continued in my lifestyle, moving farther and farther away from Him. It sounds crazy, but my illness has actually been a blessing. It brought me back to God."

Lamentations 3:33 shows us God's compassionate heart for His wayward children when Jeremiah writes, "For he does not willingly bring affliction or grief to anyone." This heart-wrenching statement reminds us that although God often allows the natural consequences of our sin to impact our lives, He doesn't delight in it.

"Though he brings grief," Lamentations 3:32 says, "he will show compassion, so great is his unfailing love."

Lena lived six more months after we reconnected. We laughed, cried, and studied God's Word together. Her body weakened, but her spirit grew stronger. Her confidence in God's greater purpose for her illness never wavered, nor did her trust in God's tender heart toward her. She knew that although her body would one day die, her spirit would live forever. And an eternity with God is infinitely better than a lifetime without Him.

Uncommon Thought
God never celebrates when the results of our disobedience wreak havoc on our lives. Instead, He weeps with us.

Unusual Faith
Have you ever struggled with events or circumstances in your or someone else's life that came about because of disobedience? Maybe this war is raging in your spirit right now. It's time to stop fighting. Talk to God. Confess and repent of any sin that is hindering your relationship with Him. Tell Him about your hurt, pain, fear, disappointment. Be honest. He knows anyway. Then take up the shield of faith. Say to Him, "No matter what happens, I will trust that you will use what you've allowed into my life for my good and your glory. Give me the faith and courage to walk the path you have set before me."

Read Lamentations 3:24–40.

Hard Conversations

"You must speak my words to them, whether they
listen or fail to listen, for they are rebellious."

EZEKIEL 2:7

My husband, David, dreaded the conversation he knew needed to take place. Steve was like a brother. They'd attended school together, played high school football, and spent hours hanging out. When Steve came to faith in Christ, David felt almost as excited as the day he'd gotten saved. He watched Steve take his first faith steps and rejoiced when Steve and his wife began studying the Bible together. His child-like faith was inspiring. Although he'd been through some dark times, Steve finally seemed to be headed in the right direction.

And then he wasn't.

First he wouldn't answer his cell phone. Then he was too busy at work to take David's calls. Days went by with no return call. Giving in to the nagging concern that weighed heavily on his heart, David finally drove by his home one evening, hoping to see his car in the driveway.

A mutual friend, similarly concerned, called David with news he never expected to hear.

Steve had quit his job, left his wife, and moved across the country with a woman he'd met at a trade show.

We don't know what made Steve answer David's call several weeks later. He'd ignored dozens of other attempts. But the conversation shed some light on what was going on, and it wasn't pretty.

After listening to Steve's story, my husband took a deep breath and said what he knew he had to say.

"I'm sorry you've been struggling, but this isn't the answer. I know you want someone to love you, and a home, and a family, but God can't bless your life when you totally disregard His principles. What you're doing is wrong, and it's not going to turn out well. Why not come home and let us help you?"

David reminded Steve of his love and—most importantly—God's love. "You'll get through this. With God's help, you can turn this ship around."

Steve hung up. We didn't hear from him for two and a half years.

As my husband grieved the loss of Steve's friendship and mourned the path he'd chosen, he wondered if things might have turned out differently if he hadn't confronted Steve about his sin.

God's words to the prophet Ezekiel reminded him of his responsibility to speak the truth, even when the message is unpopular. "You must speak my words to them, whether they listen or fail to listen, for they are rebellious" (Ezekiel 2:7).

As Christians, we've been given the privilege of sharing God's truth with those around us. We find some of this truth easy to receive. Who doesn't like hearing God loves them and wants to give them a life filled with joy and purpose?

Other parts of God's truth are hard. Not everyone wants to be reminded that the God who loves us has also established principles to help us achieve that life filled with joy and purpose and bring Him glory through our obedience.

My grandchildren are a classic example of hard truths. They

shout "Yippee!" when I walk through the door with ice cream. But they grumble when I require them to wash their hands and sit at the table to eat it. And oh, the pushback I get when I remind them that we eat sweets only in moderation.

The same is true when God prompts us to share His message. Sometimes those with whom we share receive it with gladness and thanksgiving. Other times they scorn, reject, and despise it.

The two and a half years before Steve reached out to David again were long and heartbreaking. The path he had taken was fun and exciting for a while, he told us. Before long, however, its sandy foundation began to crumble. With the broken pieces of his life piled high around him, he finally admitted his need for help. He reached out to those who loved him and began the long journey home. One of the first people he reconnected with was David.

I wish I could say Steve is following the Lord with all his heart, but I can't. Not yet, at least. But he's more open and tender, and that's a good start. When he and my husband talk, Steve knows two things are going to happen. First, David's going to remind him how much he loves him. Second, he's going to point him to God, the greatest source of help and healing.

Uncommon Thought

Our responsibility to share God's truth isn't determined by others' response. We must speak the truth in love and trust God with the results.

Unusual Faith

Do you hesitate to share God's truth with others because you're afraid of their reaction? What might happen if you don't speak the truth?

Are you willing to take that chance? Consider that God has placed you where you are because your warning, challenge, or exhortation could change someone's life. Whether they receive your words with gladness or grumbling, you can rest in the knowledge that you obeyed God. Prayerfully trust Him for the results.

Read Ezekiel 2:1–7.

DANIEL

One Reason God Answers Our Prayers

"We do not make requests of
you because we are righteous, but
because of your great mercy."

DANIEL 9:18

Ever wonder why God answers our prayers?

I used to think God answered our prayers because we were pretty good people. Until I discovered that no one's good. Not really good, by God's standard. Romans 3:23 confirms this. "For all have sinned and fall short of the glory of God."

So much for that idea.

Then I thought God might answer our prayers if we do more good than we do bad. You know, like the proverbial scales so many people use to gauge whether or not they'll go to heaven. Enough good works, and you slide in. More bad than good? Sorry. No admittance.

Since this is a faulty and unbiblical approach to eternity (Ephesians 2:8–9), I'm not sure why I thought it might apply to our prayers, but for a while I entertained the idea. Picture this . . .

God: "Ah, Lori. Now, she's done really well this week. She attended church twice, put a tithe in the offering plate, and let three people go ahead of her in line at Aldi. That deserves at least one answered prayer, don't you think?"

Unfortunately, I've found no biblical support for this view, either. While I've read hundreds of passages on how living according to God's principles will bring blessings into our lives, I found nothing that discussed the ratio of good deeds to answered prayers. God does not "owe me" a favor as a repayment for my good works.

Too bad, because there were a few prayer requests I really wanted to bargain for.

Then I considered the possibility that if I mustered up enough passion and energy about my prayer requests, then maybe my fervency would catch God's attention and convince Him I was serious. After all, doesn't James 5:16 say, "The effective, *fervent* prayer of a righteous man avails much" (NKJV, emphasis mine)?

So fervent I became.

"God, pleeeeeeeeease act in this situation. I know you are mighty, all-powerful, all-knowing, Warrior of the Universe, King of Kings and Lord of Lords, God of Abraham, Isaac, Jacob, and all the patriarchs whose names I don't remember. You're faster than a speeding bullet, stronger than a locomotive, able to leap tall buildings . . . oops, sorry. I got you confused with Superman for a minute there, but I know you're even better than Superman, so pleeeeeeeeease answer my prayer."

But the problem with this prayer theology is that it pictures God as a reluctant giver whom I must manipulate into answering my prayers. It implies that if I don't put on enough of a show, if I don't beat my breast and fall on my face, or work myself into an emotional frenzy in an attempt to convince God of my sincerity, then He won't give me what I want.

This is so not God. Matthew 7:11 tells me He loves to give good gifts to His children. Generously. Lavishly. Joyfully. I don't have to become a drama queen to demonstrate my passion. He already knows my heart—without all the theatrics.

Then I figured it out. I remembered that passage about the widow who had no other recourse but to badger the unrighteous judge until he gave in and granted her petition. That's the key. Persistence. Nag God until He's so sick of hearing my voice that He answers my prayer just to shut me up.

No. No. No. That's not it, either. While many prayer requests require a concerted effort over a period of time, God isn't a miser whose every gift must be squeezed out of His prayer-pinching hands. The purpose of persevering prayer is to change me, not God. I'm the one who needs to be conformed to His will, not Him to mine.

And then I read Daniel 9:18 and discovered one beautiful reason God answers our prayers.

"We do not make requests of you because we are righteous," Daniel prayed, "but because of your great mercy."

Our morality doesn't earn God's favor. Nor do our good works. Our fervency doesn't manipulate Him. Nor does our persistence.

God answers our prayers because of His mercy. The abundant, unmerited, gracious favor that flows out of God's great, big, loving heart. We can't earn it. We don't deserve it, but we should be infinitely grateful for it.

So the next time I pray, I'm going to approach Him on the basis of His mercy. Imagine that.

Uncommon Thought

I don't have to earn an audience with God, and I don't have to bargain or cajole Him to answer my prayers. I can rest in His mercy.

Unusual Faith

What obstacle or wrong belief hinders your prayer life? How does it compare with Scripture? As you pray today, set aside your preconceived ideas and come to God solely on the basis of His mercy.

Read Daniel 9:4–18.

Sowing Stones, Reaping Rocks

Sow righteousness for yourselves, reap the fruit
of unfailing love, and break up your unplowed
ground; for it is time to seek the LORD, until he
comes and showers his righteousness on you.

HOSEA 10:12

While my childhood friends set up lemonade stands, I considered selling rocks. Every spring my father would till our garden, and every year he'd encounter stones that hadn't been there the year before. My fanciful mind imagined gremlins tunneling beneath the soil of our snow-covered garden each winter sowing stone seeds. And every spring the ground produced a bumper crop. The beautiful stone walls that characterize New England's landscape are proof that the cash crop of this region is rocks.

"Good fences make good neighbors," Robert Frost (a New Englander) wisely said. Good fences also give you something to do with the rocks you dig out of your garden every spring.

Hosea 10:12 reminds me that if I don't tend the stony soil of my own heart, I, like my native New England, am in danger of producing a rocky crop only useful for building walls.

"Break up your unplowed ground," the Lord through Hosea calls to us. "Sow righteousness for yourselves, reap the fruit of unfailing love."

The Christian life is a series of surrenders. In the first, the Big Surrender, we yield ourselves to God in confession and repentance. We lay everything upon God's altar. Our sin. Our self-righteousness. Our independence.

After the Big Surrender comes a series of Small Surrenders—small, that is, in relation to our soul and our eternal destiny. Some are material, like the skimpy bathing suit and music I forsook when I first accepted Christ. Others are spiritual, like my tendency to worry and fret.

Little by little God tills the ground of our hearts, unearthing rocks that hinder the growth of spiritual fruit. As my family discovered in our rocky garden, nothing grows where a rock sits. It's either a stone or a tomato. Never both.

That affection for sensual books or movies? Dig it out.

The desire to gossip? Gotta go.

The tendency to hoard money instead of give generously? Out with it.

We, however, must allow God to do His work. My father couldn't remove the stones from our garden if my mother shooed him away every time he approached. God is willing, but we must submit.

Spiritual tilling begins when we invite God to do a soil check. Psalm 139:23–24 is a good prayer: "Search me, God, and know my heart; test me and know my anxious thoughts. See if there is any offensive way in me, and lead me in the way everlasting."

After we've invited the Gardener to perform a diagnostic, it's important to linger long enough to hear His report. During this period of active listening, the Lord will often bring something to my awareness. An unkind word I said. A sinful pleasure no one saw. A neglected chance to minister in His name. This is the time to confess and forsake. Otherwise, I'm like the farmer who sees a rock in his garden and looks the other way.

Rocks are amazingly persistent. We must return to our gardens daily and cooperate with the Master Gardener while He removes the rocks.

The best part of this process is God's commitment to me. While I'm free to resist Him, He promises never to leave me to myself. When I am faithless, He is faithful. Season after season, year after year, failed crop or bumper crop, He gently and persistently sifts through my life and nudges me toward righteousness.

Despite my weakness and frailty, He tills and plants, tills and plants, creating a fruitful harvest. He helps me desire what's best, changing my wants until they align with what He wants for me. My job is to cooperate, even when it's hard. Especially when it's hard. After all, why would I want to harvest a truckload of rocks when I have the potential to "reap the fruit of unfailing love"?

Uncommon Thought
God is willing to remove the stones that hinder my spiritual harvest, but I must cooperate with the process.

Unusual Faith
One of the signs of being God's children is that He changes us to be more like himself (2 Corinthians 5:17). Think back over your Christian journey. Can you see how He has changed your wants and desires?

When He brings a "rock" to your attention, do you respond defensively or humbly? Beginning today, invite Him to do a soil check. Listen to what He reveals to you, and cooperate as He removes the rocks in your life. Then you'll bear rich spiritual fruit.

Read Hosea 11:1–11.

Rending Our Hearts

"Even now," declares the LORD, "return to me
with all your heart, with fasting and weeping and
mourning." Rend your heart and not your garments.
Return to the LORD your God, for he is gracious and
compassionate, slow to anger and abounding in love.

JOEL 2:12–13

As youngsters, my sister Cindy and I would often squabble. When our voices reached a certain decibel level, my mother feared we'd come to blows, so she'd intervene. She'd listen to our heated defense of why one of us was right and the other was wrong, then declare the matter settled.

"Lori, tell your sister you're sorry."

"Sorry," I'd mutter, glaring at Cindy.

"Now, Cindy, tell Lori you're sorry."

"Sorry," she'd mumble, glaring back.

"Good," Mom would say, satisfied that she'd mediated yet another heated exchange. "Now go play."

We'd stomp out of the room, no more reconciled than when we'd begun the argument.

From my sage position as an adult, I look back on those exchanges with greater understanding. I know now that reconciliation can't happen without sorrow over sin and genuine repentance. This truth applies to both human and spiritual relationships.

I wonder sometimes if Christians, myself included, take our sin too lightly. Do we make excuses for our bad behavior, or, worse yet, fail to deal with it at all? When we sin, do we treat our offenses more casually than we should, muttering a token, "Sorry," to the sky, when true confession and repentance is needed? Do we eagerly wrap ourselves in God's blanket of forgiveness and then drag it through the mud with our sinful actions?

Today's passage from the book of Joel shares God's strong encouragement to the wayward children of Israel. "Return to me with all your heart, with fasting and weeping and mourning. Rend your heart and not your garments."

In Bible days, people expressed sorrow by tearing (rending) their clothes. Everyone who saw them knew they were grieving. If someone wanted to demonstrate their repentance and sorrow over their sin, they would publicly tear their clothes. However, similarly to my token, "I'm sorry," to my sister, the outward display didn't always mean they were sincerely repentant in their heart. When we sin against God and others, God's Word insists outward sorrow isn't enough. We must mean it on the inside.

The spiritually proper response to sin is a rending of our hearts— seeing our sin as God sees it—and humbling ourselves in confession and repentance. "Return to the LORD your God," Joel 2:13 reads, "for he is gracious and compassionate, slow to anger and abounding in love." Confession and repentance don't impact (or restore) our salvation, because Christ's atoning work on the cross settled that forever. Instead, they restore the sweet communion we enjoyed with God before sin interrupted our fellowship.

As my sister and I got older, we realized that when we genuinely felt and expressed remorse and regret over our unkind words and actions, we were able to move past the offenses and back into warm camaraderie again. God desires this process for our relationship with Him as well.

So the next time you sin (against God and others), stop a moment to reflect. Why did you do it, say it, or fail to do it? How do you think God sees it? Are you truly sorry? Then pray, expressing to God how you've offended Him. Ask for His forgiveness and help. Rend your heart, not your garment. When you do, His patient spirit and boundless love will wrap you in forgiveness and restoration.

Uncommon Thought

When we truly repent of our sin, then we can fully receive God's grace and forgiveness.

Unusual Faith

Invite God to search your heart and reveal any sin He finds there. Sit quietly until you hear from Him. When you do, confess, repent, and forsake what He's shown you. Ask Him to give you victory over whatever thought, action, or attitude He's revealed. Obey Him in whatever He shows you to do. Thank Him for His forgiveness and love.

Read Joel 2:12–17.

When Murderers Go Free

"I will not relent."

Amos 1:3

My uncle's murderer showed no mercy. Not content merely to kill him, he took careful aim while my uncle fumbled with a jammed gun, desperately trying to defend himself. The murderer shot him once in each ankle to ensure he couldn't run away, then once in each knee to add to his already excruciating pain. While my uncle writhed in agony, the man squeezed off his final shot—straight into my uncle's heart.

A slick, high-dollar lawyer mounted his defense, and my uncle's murderer never spent a night in jail. Declared innocent on grounds of self-defense, he walked free.

Appalled at such a travesty of justice, my family reeled in disbelief. How could a judicial system committed to defending the innocent and punishing the guilty allow this madman to go unpunished?

Years later, words from the Old Testament book of Amos brought me comfort. This tiny, nine-chapter book reads like a federal court docket. In it, Amos the shepherd lists the sins of Israel, Judah, and the surrounding nations:

The Lord says:

"For three sins of Damascus, even for four, I will not relent. . . .

"For three sins of Gaza, even for four, I will not relent. . . .

"For three sins of Tyre, even for four, I will not relent. . . ."

(Amos 1:3, 6, 9)

On and on the list reads, detailing the atrocities these countries had committed against each other and against the Lord—murders, cruelties, broken promises, anger, rage, violence, sexual sin, spiritual apostasy. The list extends for two long chapters.

Yet for every crime, God made a promise: "I will not relent from punishing" (Amos 1:3, 6, 9, 11, 13; 2:1, 4, 6 HCSB).

God did punish each of these nations, including Israel and Judah. But their punishment didn't come immediately. Our longsuffering God, not wanting to destroy anyone, waited. He extended undeserved mercy. He wooed them with His grace.

"Seek good and not evil so that you may live," He pleaded. "And the LORD, the God of Hosts, will be with you, as you have claimed. Hate evil and love good; establish justice in the gate. Perhaps the LORD, the God of Hosts, will be gracious" (Amos 5:14–15).

My family and I wanted immediate justice for my uncle's murderer. Instead, he was acquitted. We wanted him incarcerated for life, but he was released.

The words of Amos the prophet comforted us. They assured us that God had not turned a blind eye toward this man's crime. He wasn't looking the other way when the murderer squeezed off those shots.

God saw. God cared. And one day, if this man doesn't repent, he'll stand before a jury of one, and God will judge. No one will mount a defense, and no slick lawyer will help him go free.

"I also saw the dead, the great and the small, standing before the throne, and books were opened. Another book was opened, which is the book of life, and the dead were judged according to their works by what was written in the books" (Revelation 20:12).

In the meantime, we can wait without bitterness, knowing justice will come.

A year after my uncle's murder trial, the Lord spoke to my heart. *You need to forgive him.*

And if that wasn't hard enough . . . *and share the gospel with him.*

Realizing God was offering me the healing and freedom my bitter heart needed, I obeyed. I wrote my uncle's murderer a letter telling him how much his actions had hurt our family and how bitterness had clogged my heart.

"But I, too, am a sinner in need of forgiveness," I wrote. "As Christ has forgiven me, so I forgive you." I shared the gospel as simply as I could and ended with a plea. "My forgiveness means nothing in light of the great crime you have committed before the Lord. I pray you will confess your sins and ask Christ to save you."

As I read through the book of Amos, I realized God's longsuffering mercy toward my uncle's murderer had given me time to extend my forgiveness and tell him how he could receive ultimate forgiveness—the kind only God the righteous Judge can bestow. I pray he accepted it.

Now it's your turn. Who has hurt, killed, or destroyed something precious in your life? Rest assured, God knows your pain. He sees the sins that have been committed against you. Nothing escapes His all-seeing eyes. You can rest in peace, knowing judgment will come. When it does, it will be just.

In the meantime, keep your heart from bitterness, extend forgiveness, and pray that God will use even your pain to bring himself glory.

Uncommon Thought
God will, in His perfect timing and righteousness, judge every one of the wrongs committed against you. You can trust Him to do what's right.

Unusual Faith
Examine your heart. Is there any bitterness there? Confess it to God and ask Him to set you free. As an act of obedience, pray for the person who has sinned against you.

Read Amos 1–2.

The Tricky Part about Being Deceived

The pride of your heart has deceived you.

OBADIAH 1:3

"The tricky part about being deceived," my pastor-husband often says, "is that you don't know you're deceived."

I see this truth play itself out all the time. Late at night, when the house is quiet and my thoughts run to every corner of the globe, I think about Katie, who's living with her boyfriend. She thinks the institution of marriage isn't necessary to have a committed and fulfilling relationship. She's deceived and doesn't know it.

I think about Joseph, who used to believe in God, but after his father, who was caring for his handicapped mother, died in a car wreck, he's not so sure. He thinks having no God would be better than having a God who allows bad things to happen. He's deceived and doesn't know it.

I think about Jackie, who's bored with her marriage and not sure she loves her husband anymore. Did she marry the wrong person? Maybe there's someone else out there who could make her happy. Life would be better if she left and started over. She's deceived and doesn't know it.

And I think about myself, who worries about the past, the present, and the future. I'm not always convinced God knows what's best for me and my family. I struggle to trust. I lay weighty burdens on His altar, then snatch them off again to worry and fret over them some more. I'm deceived and don't know it.

The Old Testament prophet Obadiah described the all-too-common state of being deceived in his tiny, one-chapter book. Only twenty-one verses long, this vignette of a book can't go nose-to-nose with tomes such as Isaiah or Jeremiah, yet it makes a significant contribution to Scripture. By the third verse, Obadiah nails the root of most human deception—our pride.

Notice I say *our* pride—because none of us is exempt. I didn't list the people I mentioned above so I could point out how *wrong* they are and how *right* I am. Pride has been deceiving humanity since Adam and Eve sinned in the garden.

In Adam and Eve's pride, they assumed they knew better than God what would make them happy. Surely God was holding out on them, they reasoned. And if He was going to withhold something good from them, they'd have to usurp His authority and claim it for themselves. They were deceived and didn't know it.

Humanity has been following Adam and Eve's example ever since. Anytime we come to a crossroads and have to choose between our way and God's way, humility and pride go head-to-head. Pride often wins.

Pride tricks us into thinking we can't trust God to work in our lives for our good and His glory. It tells us God-given institutions like marriage and the church aren't necessary for a healthy and happy world. Pride tells us that if *we* were God, we'd never allow sickness, pain, or death into the world. It forgets that the world God designed had none of these things until humanity exercised its prideful free will and chose sin instead of the Savior.

Pride tells us to run from a loveless marriage and deceives us into thinking our relationship is too broken to fix. Worse yet, it convinces us that if we could just *find* the right person instead of working to *become* the right person, marriage would be effortless and problem-free.

Prideful deception lies and tells us when things get hard, God must be on vacation. If He loved us, pride whispers, we'd never experience pain, loss, or difficulty. We reason hard times can't produce anything good. We withdraw our trust and deposit it in the bank of worry and despair.

But, glory hallelujah, a cure has been found. The antidote to pride is humility. A humble heart acknowledges that even when we don't understand God's ways, we can trust His character. Humility works at a marriage where love has grown cold, believing God can restore and rebuild it. And a humble heart submits our lives to God's all-knowing and all-loving will, trusting that He will work in everything for our good and His glory.

This is what a humble heart looks like—and a humble heart will never deceive us.

Uncommon Thought

Anytime we come to a crossroads and have to choose between our way and God's way, humility and pride go head-to-head—and pride often wins.

Unusual Faith

What's one area of your life in which you're struggling to believe that God's way is better than your way? Talk to God about it. Ask Him to show you if pride might be keeping you from trusting Him. Invite Him to show you that His word is best—through His Word; wise counsel; and His still, small voice in your heart. Write down what you've heard in a journal, then take a step of faith to demonstrate your trust.

Read Obadiah 1:1–21.

Mercy in Disguise

Those who regard worthless idols
forsake their own Mercy.
JONAH 2:8 (NKJV)

Does anyone *not* know the story of Jonah? Rebellious prophet catches the first ship headed south after God calls him north to preach to the wicked Ninevites. A storm arises, threatening the ship and all those on board. Jonah confesses his sin, offers his life in exchange for the crew's, and urges the sailors to toss him overboard.

But instead of drowning, Jonah gets swallowed by a great fish, who just happens to be swimming toward Nineveh. Jonah repents of his rebellious ways, the fish burps him out, and he heads toward the city center, preaching repentance as he goes. The city responds, and they all live happily ever after. The End.

If you ask someone, "Who gets saved in the book of Jonah?" they'll respond, "Why, the Ninevites, of course." Every kid in children's church knows this. Jonah shines as an ambassador of God's mercy toward the disobedient, unbelieving Ninevites. But hidden in the first chapter, we find something unexpected—glistening examples of God's mercy toward Jonah, toward a disobedient, believing Hebrew.

The first glimmer of God's mercy toward Jonah comes in the form of a storm. "The LORD sent a great wind on the sea, and such a violent storm arose that the ship threatened to break up" (Jonah 1:4).

Jonah recognized it for what it was—a divine response to his sin. "I know that it is my fault that this great storm has come upon you," he told his shipmates (v. 12). But he was wrong about God's intent. Jonah assumed the storm was meant to kill him as punishment for disobeying God's call to go to Nineveh. And he was willing to accept his sentence. But he wasn't willing to take the entire crew with him. He instructed the sailors, "Pick me up and throw me into the sea . . . and it will become calm."

They did. And it did.

Jonah was a dead man. He knew it and the sailors knew it. As they threw him overboard, they prayed to God, "Please, LORD, do not let us die for taking this man's life" (v. 14).

But God didn't send the powerful storm to destroy Jonah. He sent it to save him. How do we know this? Because Jonah didn't drown. God sent the storm to save Jonah from himself.

As he sank into the depths of the sea, God extended His mercy a second time. Instead of wind and waves, God sent a fish. "Now the LORD provided a huge fish to swallow Jonah" (v. 17).

In Jonah's mind, his situation went from bad to worse, but we know better. Instead of becoming fish bait, Jonah became a passenger in the world's first submarine. God used the great fish to shelter and transport Jonah back to a place of repentance and restoration.

But Jonah's repentance wasn't instantaneous. While he should have been praising God for his unlikely rescue, he sat with his arms crossed in the pitch-black belly of the fish for three days and three nights. Floating in gastric juices and breathing the stench of rotting fish carcasses, he resisted God's mercy and clung to his worthless idols of prejudice, superiority, and rebellion.

Until a light dawned.

"When my life was ebbing away," Jonah prayed, "I remembered you, LORD, and my prayer rose to you, to your holy temple" (Jonah 2:7).

"And the LORD commanded the fish, and it vomited Jonah onto dry land" (v. 10).

As Christians, we all have our Jonah moments. We sense God's call and run the other way. Fear, prejudice, a lack of faith, or a school of other excuses hinder us from obeying what we know He wants us to do.

Because He's committed to helping us grow and bear spiritual fruit, He orders the circumstances of our lives to give us every opportunity to turn back to himself. What looks like punishment might instead be the velvet glove of mercy.

When we return to Him, He'll again work through us to bless other people. We may not see an entire city come to faith in God like Jonah did, but we can be confident He'll use us to accomplish His good and perfect will in the lives of those around us.

Uncommon Thought
What looks like judgment may instead be God's mercy in disguise.

Unusual Faith
As you look back on the difficult seasons of your life, have you ever considered the possibility that God may have allowed those times to draw you closer to himself or to redirect your steps? Could what looked like punishment instead have been a manifestation of His mercy?

What about your life now? Are you walking in obedience to God, or are you running in the opposite direction? Have you been reluctant to obey something He's called you to do? Demonstrate your faith by saying yes today.

Read the entire book of Jonah. (It's only four chapters.)

Spiritual Blindness

Though I sit in darkness, the LORD will be my light.

MICAH 7:8

My friend Thom is going blind. Although he was born sighted, a destructive eye disease is progressively reducing his sight to shapes and shadows. Soon his vision will be completely gone.

Resourceful and smart, Thom has learned to adapt. He works with assistive technology to help other visually-impaired people access resources and tools. He walks in the neighborhood, shops at the grocery store near his home, and recently tried his hand at custom cabinetry, building a beautiful, functional pantry in his kitchen. He and his wife, Tracy, who was born blind, taught me how to use my new pressure cooker and often share recipes.

I admire Thom's spiritual curiosity. He thinks deeply about things and asks insightful questions. The New Testament stories of Jesus's miracles are especially interesting to him.

One Sunday, a few weeks before Christmas, he surprised us. Rising from his pew and walking confidently to the front of the church, he accepted the microphone from our music director. Turning to face the congregation, he began to sing, "Mary, Did You Know?"

As he sang through the list of miracles Christ had performed during His time on earth, God gave me insight into one of the reasons Jesus is so dear to Thom—and why the promise of heaven is so sweet. Thom knows that a time will come again, just as in the days of Christ's ministry, when the deaf will hear, the lame will walk, and, yes, the blind will see.

In this lifetime, Thom sits in increasing darkness. With his limited vision, his perspective grows darker. But despite his physical blindness, Thom "sees" better than most, because the Lord has opened his spiritual eyes.

"Though I sit in darkness," Micah 7:8 reads, "the LORD will be my light."

In God's wonderful providence, Thom's hope is our hope as well. While most of us don't suffer from physical blindness, we often fall prey to spiritual blindness. Our vision becomes clouded, our perspective grows confused, and we sometimes lose our way.

"Because I have sinned against him," Micah confessed, "I will bear the LORD's wrath, until he pleads my case and upholds my cause" (7:9).

Physical blindness is often incurable. Not so with spiritual blindness. Micah describes how God the Great Physician heals the spiritually blind: "He will bring me out into the light; I will see his righteousness" (7:9). When God shines the light of Christ on our sins, we're able to view them against the backdrop of His righteousness. We realize that offering up our best works in an attempt to earn His favor is as effective as a blind man groping in the darkness trying to find his way out of a burning building.

Like my friend Thom, we must cry out to God, admit our need, and humble ourselves before Him. When we accept the gift of forgiveness made possible by Jesus's death on the cross, our eyes are opened, and we marvel, "Who is a God like you, who pardons sin and forgives . . . ? You do not stay angry forever but delight to show mercy" (7:18). Whether we're coming to Christ the first time for salvation, or repenting of a besetting sin that hinders our fellowship, God's arms are always open to welcome us home.

One of the reasons Thom looks forward to heaven is because he knows his sight will be restored. But he doesn't have to wait until he dies to see with his spiritual eyes. God has revealed himself to Thom in ways that don't require physical sight to understand. He promises to do the same for you, and me, and everyone who turns toward Him.

When we turn our spiritual eyes toward God, we can joyfully say with the prophet Micah, "But as for me, I watch in hope for the LORD, I wait for God my Savior" (7:7).

Uncommon Thought
God promises to lift the spiritual blinders from our eyes and shine His light into the dark places. All we have to do is call upon Him.

Unusual Faith
If you are spiritually blind, stumbling through life without meaning, purpose, or direction, Christ offers to bring light into the darkness of your life. Pray, confess your sin, and surrender your life to Him. If you know Christ as Savior but find yourself blinded by the darkness of uncertainty, apathy, or fear, ask God to open your eyes to see how He's working all around you. Search His Word for insight, and apply what you learn by faith.

Read Micah 7:1–20.

Is God a Two-Faced Judge?

The LORD is a jealous and avenging God; the
LORD takes vengeance and is filled with wrath.

NAHUM 1:2

My friend Molly and her family experienced the most heartbreaking year of their lives. One night her sister, a manager at a local sandwich shop, was shot and killed in an attempted robbery as she closed the restaurant. The case was finally coming to trial. When the court assigned a judge, their attorney called them with the news.

"Some judges are unpredictable," he said, "but this judge has an excellent record. He's tough, but fair. Not swayed by legal theatrics or emotional appeals. He has a reputation for enforcing the law and upholding justice."

Molly and her family knew the final verdict was in God's hands, but with a righteous judge on the case, they were confident the men who had taken their loved one's life would be punished.

In our judicial system, we expect our public servants to uphold the law in a consistent, unbiased way. Yet many people struggle with the thought that God reigns over the earth as the ultimate judge. They stumble over Old Testament passages like Nahum 1:2 that describe God as vengeful and filled with wrath. The Bible tells us that because God is holy, no one who isn't perfect can live forever with Him in heaven. Ultimately, sin must be punished. God set the standard as ruler and creator of our world, and He has the right to enforce it.

But within every book of the Bible that describes God's obligation to punish sin and those who commit it, we also find verses that describe how much He loves and cares for those who place their faith in Him. Listen to Nahum 1:7: "The Lord is good, a refuge in times of trouble. He cares for those who trust in him."

God sees two types of people—enemies and friends. Neither group is perfect or sinless, one group turns their backs on Him and lives by their own standard. The other turns toward Him for salvation and seeks to live by His standard.

God takes "vengeance on his foes and vents his wrath against his enemies" (Nahum 1:2) but "cares for those who trust in him" (Nahum 1:7). See the difference? His wrath and judgment rightfully fall on His enemies (those who have rejected Him as Savior and Lord), and His love and care extend to His friends (those who have trusted in Christ for salvation).

Many fail to understand that God's justice is one of the greatest expressions of His love. Imagine a world with no standard for right and wrong. Consider Molly and her family. Without God's standard, they'd have no hope or expectation of just punishment for the men who killed her sister. And even if our earthly judicial system fails, they have the comfort of knowing ultimate justice will prevail. Nahum 1:3 reads, "The Lord will not leave the guilty unpunished."

One day, according to God's Word, the books will be opened in heaven. Those who have rejected God's offer of salvation through His Son, Jesus, will face the punishment they have chosen—the full and just expression of God's wrath. Those who have acknowledged their sinfulness and accepted Jesus's willingness to die in their place will find their refuge in God. They will experience God's goodness and care.

These truths accurately reflect the two faces of the God of the universe—the righteous judge and the merciful Father. While both aspects of His character are necessary, they're often misunderstood. I'm so grateful His mercy expunges our guilt, and He freely invites us to call Him our friend.

The next time you struggle with these two aspects of God's character, remember the book of Nahum. Refer to it as an example of how God compassionately balances the twin weights of justice and mercy.

Uncommon Thought
God's commitment to justice opened the door for His greatest act of love—sending Jesus to take the punishment we deserve.

Unusual Faith
Like Molly's family, we've all been wronged in some way. Large offense or small, are you willing to surrender the wrongs committed against you to God? To trust Him to bring about justice, either in this world or in the next? If the person who has hurt you isn't a Christian, will you take a giant leap of faith and begin to pray for their salvation? If they are, pray for God to work in their life.

Read Nahum 1:1–15.

Even Strong Ones Grow Weary

I will stand at my watch and station myself on the
ramparts; I will look to see what he will say to me.

HABAKKUK 2:1

You know who you are. You're the strong one.

The one others turn to when they're struggling. The one who always has a verse ready to bolster your friends' faith because you read your Bible every morning.

You're the one who carries a multitude of prayer requests close to your heart and prays for them in the night watches. And the one who reminds others that God loves them and will meet their needs, even when the situation seems impossible.

You're the one who sets the example for others to follow. Your life is a demonstration of what it looks like to rejoice in suffering, persevere through trials, and never stop believing.

But sometimes even you grow weary. It's hard being strong.

When my daughter was young and her little legs would tire, she'd tug on my husband's sleeve and whimper, "I'm tired, Daddy. Carry me."

Without missing a step, my husband would reach down and scoop her up in his big, strong arms. She'd wrap her tiny arms around his neck, tuck her head under his chin, and sigh.

"I've got you, baby girl," he'd whisper in her ear. "Take a little rest. Daddy will carry you."

If you're usually strong, but you're feeling weary right now, it's okay.

Even strong ones grow tired. It's human to wonder, Who will carry me while I carry all the others?

The prophet Habakkuk, a strong man with strong faith, also felt the strain. For years he'd watched while his beloved nation turned its back on God. Time after time he'd warned them, begging them to return. He knew there'd be an end to God's patience. His mercy would be replaced by His judgment. As a committed follower of the Lord, Habakkuk's heart ached for his countrymen.

In his weariness, he sought the Lord. "I will stand at my watch and station myself on the ramparts; I will look to see what he will say to me" (Habakkuk 2:1). In Bible times, watchmen positioned themselves on high towers in the city wall. They scanned the horizon for potential threats and waited for incoming messages.

Habakkuk, as a prophet of the LORD, figuratively did both. He watched for and warned the people of spiritual danger, and he delivered God's messages. As he lifted his lament to the Lord concerning his country's decline, God spoke to him. He reminded Habakkuk that no matter what happened, "The Lord is in his holy temple" (2:20). God was on His throne, and Habakkuk could trust Him.

Reassured of God's love and care, Habakkuk declared, "The Sovereign LORD is my strength" (3:19). Like Habakkuk, we, too can rest in God's strength when ours is gone.

If you're feeling the spiritual strain of caring for others and you don't know if you can carry on, don't be afraid to cry out to the Lord, "I'm tired, Daddy. Carry me."

Without missing a step, He'll scoop you up in His big, strong arms, tuck your head under His chin, and whisper in your ear, "I've got you, baby girl. Take a little rest. Daddy will carry you."

If you're a strong one, remember: The Sovereign Lord is your strength.

Uncommon Thought

When you grow weary, and the faith burdens you carry grow too heavy, remember: God is carrying you.

Unusual Faith

What burdens weigh you down? What sorrow, or fear, or need makes you cry when no one's looking? What situation do you carry that's too heavy for you to bear? Identify what it is (perhaps it's several things), and write them on a sheet of paper. Then give them to God in prayer.

After you've rested before the Lord and allowed Him to carry you for a while, return to your post. Determine to serve Him with the strength only He can supply. Press on, faithful one.

Read Habakkuk 2:1–4.

Will Jesus Really Return?

"I will . . . punish those who are complacent . . . who
think, 'The LORD will do nothing, either good or bad.'"

ZEPHANIAH 1:12

When Jesus walked the earth, He made a promise to His disciples:
"And if I go and prepare a place for you, I will come back and take
you to be with me that you also may be where I am" (John 14:3).

Angels confirmed His promise after His ascension. "'Men of
Galilee,' they said, 'why do you stand here looking into the sky? This
same Jesus, who has been taken from you into heaven, will come back
in the same way you have seen him go into heaven'" (Acts 1:11).
Scripture is replete with warnings and promises of God's future return to judge those who have rejected Him and reward those who
have put their trust in Him.

Yet over two thousand years have passed since Jesus walked the
earth. Twenty centuries. More than 700,500 days. If you break it down
into hours and minutes? It seems like an eternity.

False prophets have predicted the day and time of the Lord's
coming for millennia. People have sold everything they had, convinced that His return was imminent. Bible scholars have watched the
course of history and world events, sure that the dark days in which
they lived were the prophesied last days.

And every one of them has been wrong. Time marches on, uninterrupted by the much-anticipated heavenly shout.

Scoffers have also been watching the church's eager yearning for Christ's return. In Old Testament days, the prophet Zephaniah recorded God's warning to those who doubted the certainty of God's coming judgment: "I will . . . punish those who are complacent . . . who think, 'The LORD will do nothing, either good or bad'" (Zephaniah 1:12).

The apostle Peter predicted the times in which we live when he wrote, "Above all, you must understand that in the last days scoffers will come, scoffing and following their own evil desires. They will say, 'Where is this "coming" he promised?'" (2 Peter 3:3–4).

But what about us? Those who love Jesus and long for His appearing? Don't we grow weary too? Doesn't a tiny worm of doubt wiggle in the back of our minds sometimes? What if He really isn't coming back? What if it's all a delusion? What if this world is all there is?

When doubts like this come, God's Word bolsters our faith. To the complacent of Zephaniah's day, God promised, "The great day of the LORD is near—near and coming quickly" (Zephaniah 1:14). This prophecy was partially fulfilled in the destruction of Jerusalem and the capture of the Israelites by the Babylonians. Its total fulfillment remains on the horizon when God will return to judge the living and the dead. Until then, we can rest in the truth that "he who promised is faithful" (Hebrews 10:23).

"At that time," God promises, "I will gather you; at that time I will bring you home" (Zephaniah 3:20). We can take heart from this, resting in the assurance that when He comes, we'll be right there with Him.

What a day that will be.

Uncommon Thought

The Lord's return is two thousand years closer than when Christ walked the earth. Will He come in our lifetime? I don't know. But no matter *when* He comes, we can rest in God's promises that He *will* come.

Unusual Faith

Do you wonder sometimes if Christ really will return? One of the ways we can seek God in our doubt and discouragement is through His Word. Because He knew we'd grow weary, He gave us more than three times as many promises concerning Christ's second coming than He did His first. And since every prophecy was fulfilled concerning His first coming, we have no reason to doubt the promises that point to His second coming. They warn us, encourage us, and give us hope. Why not do a search of some of the prophecies concerning Christ's return and claim them as promises in prayer? Spending time in God's Word is an effective way to strengthen our faith.

Read Zephaniah 3:1–20.

HAGGAI

A Purse with Holes in It

Now this is what the LORD Almighty says: "Give
careful thought to your ways. You have planted
much, but harvested little. You eat, but never have
enough. You drink, but never have your fill. You
put on clothes, but are not warm. You earn wages,
only to put them in a purse with holes in it."

HAGGAI 1:5–6

"We never seem to get ahead," Rebecca said. "Without fail, as soon
as we have any money saved, the washing machine breaks, someone
gets sick, or we get a flat tire." Tears welled up in her eyes. "John took
a second job working weekends, but instead of having more money,
we have less." She lifted wide eyes to meet mine. "I don't know how
much longer we can go on like this."

Financial struggles are real—and frightening. Sadly, Rebecca's
story isn't unique. Most of us, at one time or another, have struggled
to pay the bills, provide for the kids, and save for the future. And while
lean times come to us all, some couples always fight to stay afloat.

In the tiny Old Testament book of Haggai, we find an eloquent
description of a community struggling with the problem of too much
month at the end of their money.

"Now this is what the LORD Almighty says: 'Give careful thought to your ways. You have planted much, but harvested little. You eat, but never have enough. You drink, but never have your fill. You put on clothes, but are not warm. You earn wages, only to put them in a purse with holes in it'" (Haggai 1:5–6).

A purse with holes in it. Wow. That's quite a word picture.

Financial problems are complex, with no simple answers. But many overlook a biblical principle—each of us should be giving to God's work. Such was the case with the Israelites.

"You expected much," the Lord said, "but see, it turned out to be little. What you brought home, I blew away. Why? . . . Because of my house, which remains a ruin, while each of you is busy with your own house" (v. 9).

Concerned more about building their houses and securing their livelihood, the Israelites had neglected God and His work. This is also the case with many families today.

"We'll give to the church after we pay off our debts."

"We can't afford to give right now. The cable bill's two months past due, and I have to pay club fees for the kids' travel ball team."

"Let the rich members support the missionaries. They have plenty of money."

God, however, has a different perspective on giving, saving, and spending. "So do not worry, saying, 'What shall we eat?' or 'What shall we drink?' or 'What shall we wear?' For the pagans run after all these things, and your heavenly Father knows that you need them. But seek first his kingdom and his righteousness, and all these things will be given to you as well" (Matthew 6:31–33).

These simple verses provide the key to biblical stewardship:

Don't worry.

Give God a portion of your time, talent, and resources.

Trust Him to provide what you need.

The Israelites of Haggai's day (and many Christians today) had it backward. Their approach looked more like this:

Worry.

Stop giving to God.

Do whatever it takes to maintain our lifestyle.

When Rebecca and her husband hit a wall, they wisely sought biblical financial counseling. Their advisor suggested a plan to help them get back on their feet. He encouraged them to develop a budget, eliminate unnecessary and luxury spending, and dedicate a portion of their income to the Lord's work.

Although giving away a portion of their money seemed counterintuitive, as they stepped out in faith, they saw God multiply the remaining funds and stretch them further than they ever thought possible.

Rebecca's family's financial situation didn't turn around immediately, but with hard work, prayer, and self-control, they now enjoy a comfortable, debt-free life. Best of all, they eagerly share with other struggling couples how God met them where they were and provided for them in ways they never could have imagined.

Uncommon Thought

God meets the needs of His children in awe-inspiring ways when they commit to honor Him first.

Unusual Faith

Take an honest look at your financial stewardship. Does it most closely resemble Haggai 1:5–6 or Matthew 6:33? Ask God to help you seek His kingdom first as you choose how to spend your time, talent, and resources.

Read Haggai 1:1–15.

ZECHARIAH

It Doesn't Get Any Better than This—Or Does It?

"I myself will be a wall of fire around [Jerusalem],"
declares the LORD, "and I will be its glory within."

ZECHARIAH 2:5

I can only imagine what it would be like to watch enemy invaders ransack and pillage my beloved homeland. Or burn my place of worship to the ground—the place where my babies were dedicated, my children were taught, and my loved ones were laid to rest. I can't imagine the anguish I'd feel if pagan marauders rounded up my friends and family, abused us, and forced us to march thousands of miles to a land not our own. Even worse, how would it feel to know that we had brought this destruction upon ourselves?

Like a recurring nightmare, these memories played again and again in the minds of the Israelites. They were now living in exile in Babylon during the fifth century BC. Despite God's repeated warnings, they'd turned their backs on Him and followed after pagan gods. God had no other choice but to judge them, knowing He couldn't allow His chosen people to drag His holy name through the mud of idolatry. With a heavy heart, He allowed Nebuchadnezzar's conquering army to ravage their land and carry them off.

But now the seventy-year exile was ending. God's Spirit was stirring in the hearts of His people and speaking through prophets like Zechariah.

"Return to me," the Lord said to His people, "and I will return to you. . . . I will return to Jerusalem with mercy, and there my house will be rebuilt. . . . Jerusalem will be a city without walls" (Zechariah 1:3, 16; 2:4).

And then the sweetest promise: "'I myself will be a wall of fire around it,' declares the LORD, 'and I will be its glory within'" (v. 5).

A wall of fire around it.

Because every word in the Bible is inspired and purposeful, I suspect God chose this word picture to remind the Israelites of their ancestors' exodus from Egypt. When the Egyptian army pursued and threatened to overtake them, God placed His glory cloud between them. This pillar of cloud and red-hot fire, a glimpse of His holiness, kept them safe from harm.

Now, hundreds of years later, He again promised to stand guard around them. The protective wall that had surrounded Jerusalem in the past would be absent, but God's fiery presence would take its place.

But God wasn't there simply to protect them. In the second half of verse 5, He extends an even sweeter and more precious promise: "and I will be its glory within." Not only would God surround His people, He would live in the city among them.

Can you imagine what these words meant to the Israelites after seventy years of exile in Babylon?

But it gets even better.

God's protection and presence are ours to claim, too, but after Jesus ascended into heaven, He also sent the gift of the Holy Spirit—appearing at Pentecost as tongues of fire—to permanently indwell every believer.

Sadly, the Israelites failed to learn from their seventy-year exile for idolatry and apostasy. In 70 AD, under the emperor Nero, Jerusalem and its temple were again destroyed. God's chosen people were scattered to the far reaches of the Roman Empire. For almost two millennia, they lived as aliens and strangers throughout the world.

But for us, His adopted children, God's protection continues to surround us like a wall of fire, and His glory shines—not *within the temple*, but *within us*. Our bodies have become God's permanent dwelling place through the gift of the Holy Spirit.

One day soon, God will wipe the world's slate clean and begin again with a new heaven and a new earth. Sickness, sin, sorrow, pain, and death will be permanently destroyed. We who have placed our faith in Christ will receive resurrected bodies and will experience the presence of God inside us and all around us. Wow.

It doesn't get any better than that.

Uncommon Thought

We, as children of God grafted into the family of God, have an even greater promise than the Israelites. God *with* us became God *in* us.

Unusual Faith

Ponder the implications of God's permanent presence within you in the person of the Holy Spirit. What difference does it make that God is always with you? How should His presence affect our faith, confidence, courage, boldness, and peace? The next time you encounter a frightening or overwhelming situation, remind yourself that God is not only *with* you, He is *in* you. Then walk in the confidence this truth brings.

Read Zechariah 2:1–13.

Kitchen-Sink Soup

"When you bring blind animals for sacrifice, is that
not wrong? When you sacrifice lame or diseased
animals, is that not wrong? Try offering them to
your governor! Would he be pleased with you?
Would he accept you?" says the LORD Almighty.

MALACHI 1:8

Friends of ours had a weekly tradition. After a busy week, no one felt much like cooking, so they designated Friday night as Kitchen-Sink Soup Night. Whichever parent arrived home first pulled out all the leftovers from the refrigerator. Everything that could be safely eaten was dumped into a big pot.

That half-serving of spaghetti and meat sauce? In the pot. The corn and peas from last night's meal? Toss 'em in. The roast and vegetables from the Crock-Pot dinner two days ago? In they go.

Then the chef of the day would assess the eclectic mix and decide what it needed. If it looked more like chili, they added a can of tomatoes and some chili powder. If it looked more like vegetable soup, they'd add broth and the appropriate seasonings.

With no recipe to guide the process, the results were different every time. The concoction was seldom tasty enough to invite company to join them, but as long as they didn't waste leftovers and no one had to prepare a full meal from scratch, Kitchen-Sink Soup Night was a success.

The people of Malachi's day would have wholeheartedly embraced the concept of Kitchen-Sink Soup Night. They were masters at serving up leftovers. Sadly, however, they didn't reserve their leftovers for immediate family. Instead, they kept the best for themselves and offered God the leftovers.

Before Christ made atonement for our sin on the cross, Old Testament law required the Israelites to offer animal sacrifices on the temple altar. God gave them very specific instructions about what type of animal He would accept: only young, unblemished, perfect specimens. "'For I am a great king,' says the LORD Almighty, 'and my name is to be feared among the nations'" (Malachi 1:14).

But the Israelites didn't respect God. Instead of wholeheartedly and reverently following Him, they scorned His instructions and treated Him with contempt. Listen to His charge against them:

> "When you offer blind animals for sacrifice, is that not wrong?
> When you sacrifice lame or diseased animals, is that not wrong?
> Try offering them to your governor! Would he be pleased with
> you? Would he accept you?" says the LORD Almighty. (v. 8)

Like Kitchen-Sink Soup Night, they gave God their leftovers. In a most unholy coup, they dethroned God from His rightful place as King of their lives and replaced Him with themselves. All that mattered was their comfort, their luxury, and their prosperity.

As a result, God warned, "I will send a curse on you, and I will curse your blessings" (2:2).

It's easy to look down our self-righteous noses at the arrogant, self-centered Israelites—until we examine our own lives through the lens of Scripture. Matthew 6:21 gives us a magnifying glass with which we can search our hearts: "For where your treasure is, there your heart will be also."

With this Scripture as our standard, we must ask ourselves,

Do I give God the leftovers of my energy? Do I serve Him only when it's convenient and doesn't require giving up something else I enjoy? Am I willing to be inconvenienced for Him?

Do I give God the leftovers of my money? Do I donate to God's church and ministry only after I've met all my needs (and wants)? Or do I regularly and sacrificially give to missions? The poor? The less-fortunate?

Do I give God the leftovers of my attention? Do I read His Word only after I check social media, watch TV, or hang out with friends—if I'm not too tired? Do I rush through my prayers, content to dump a wish list in God's lap and run without stopping to listen for His response?

Where are we spending our treasure? Are we giving God our very best?

It's easy to become complacent in our service to the Lord. We dine on filet mignon and lobster and serve Him the Kitchen-Sink Soup of our lives. But He deserves so much more. He is a great God, a loving God, a God who sacrificed His most precious Son on our behalf. Isn't He worthy of our very best?

Uncommon Thought
If God gave me His best, shouldn't I give Him mine?

Unusual Faith

In each of the areas of energy, money, and attention, identify one way you can give God your best this week. Write your thoughts here as a prayer commitment to the Lord, then set an early-morning reminder in your phone for the next seven days to help you implement your ideas.

Read Malachi 1:6–14.

Glory Days

"Jerusalem, Jerusalem, you who kill the prophets and
stone those sent to you, how often I have longed to
gather your children together, as a hen gathers her
chicks under her wings, and you were not willing.
Look, your house is left to you desolate. For I tell
you, you will not see me again until you say, 'Blessed
is he who comes in the name of the Lord.'"

MATTHEW 23:37–39

We laughed until we couldn't breathe. It had been years since I'd seen
Lara, but a delayed connecting flight in our city had left her with a few
hours to kill. She'd called from the airport and invited me to meet her
for a cup of coffee.

Lara had been a mentor and friend in the early days of my faith
walk. She'd given me rides to church, taught me the Bible, and challenged me to apply what I learned to my life.

I watched how she and her husband interacted. They were the
first Christian couple I knew, so I studied them closely. I'd never before known a couple that asked for forgiveness after a fight and prayed
together when they faced a decision.

"Those were good days," she said wistfully as we reminisced.
"Glory days." Then her eyes filled with tears as she lifted the cup of

coffee to her lips. "I never imagined things could go so wrong."

She told me how busyness, selfishness, and the cares of this world had crowded out the time she'd dedicated to pursuing God. As the glow of her new faith dimmed, she'd put other priorities ahead of Him. A busy season at work caused her to miss church. Her son's practice schedule interfered with her Bible study. Conflict with her husband hurt and discouraged her. She found herself praying less rather than more. Now, twenty years later, she couldn't remember the last time she'd shared her faith with someone.

"The presence of God is gone from my life," she confessed, "and I don't know how to get it back."

Lara's story is a lot like the nation of Israel's. They'd begun well. They'd marched triumphantly out of Egypt, crossed the Red Sea on dry ground, and conquered the promised land. Eventually, however, the Israelites grew cold in their commitment to God. They stopped worshiping the one true God to chase after other gods. The glory of the Lord had departed, leaving them with no manifestation of God in their midst. Ezekiel 11:23 describes how God's Shekinah glory left their temple and stood on the Mount of Olives—right in front of them. And they never even noticed.

The New Testament book of Matthew continues to describe Israel as a nation lost in the spiritual wilderness. Christ had preached the gospel of forgiveness to the multitudes, healed the sick, lame, and demon-possessed, and trained His disciples. The glory of God had walked among them for three years, yet most were still wandering "like sheep without a shepherd" (Matthew 9:36).

And now, once again, the glory of God was preparing to leave. "Jerusalem, Jerusalem, you who kill the prophets and stone those sent to you, how often I have longed to gather your children together, as a hen gathers her chicks under her wings, and you were not willing. Look, your house is left to you desolate. For I tell you, you will not see me again until you say, 'Blessed is he who comes in the name of the Lord'" (Matthew 23:37–39).

The glory of God, in the person of Jesus, again left the temple and went to the Mount of Olives, this time to pray. His path led to Golgotha, where He died a cruel death on a Roman cross. "Without the shedding of blood there is no forgiveness," the law said (Hebrews 9:22). Christ paid the penalty, making a way for sinful mankind to have a relationship with its sinless Creator.

"You may feel like the presence of God has gone from your life," I told Lara that day in the airport, "but God hasn't. When you confessed your sin and asked Christ to be your Savior, the glory of God came to live inside you. Nothing can ever take that away.

"God knew we'd wander away. That we'd fail Him. That we'd mess up. And He made provision for that. First John 1:9 says, 'If we confess our sin, he is faithful and just and will forgive us our sins and purify us from all unrighteousness.'"

"Thanks," Lara said. "I needed to hear this."

Before Lara left we laughed some more, swapped stories about our kids, and prayed together. "Lord," I said, "make us women of faith who love you so much that the light of your glory can't help but shine through us."

Uncommon Thought
The way back to God is the same path that brought you to Him. Confess your sin. Ask Him to forgive you. He's right there, waiting to gather you in His arms as a hen gathers her chicks.

Unusual Faith

Can you look back to a time when you served God wholeheartedly, with passion, and commitment, and joy? That view doesn't have to remain in the rearview mirror. You can turn the car around. If you've wandered (or slipped) away from the Lord, or perhaps you've grown lukewarm, talk to God about it. Once you make the first move toward Him, He will run to meet you.

If you're enjoying a season of closeness with God, do everything you can to keep your zeal and excitement. Guard your times of Bible reading and prayer. Don't allow busyness or laziness to squeeze them out. Consider reading a new translation of the Bible, listening to an audio Bible on your phone, or beginning a new study to keep things fresh.

Read Matthew 23:1–12.

MARK

Are We Hiding Jesus?

He entered a house and did not want
anyone to know it; yet he could not
keep his presence a secret.

MARK 7:24

When I was a young mother, I hid chocolate from my children.

I had good reasons, chief among them that I needed a mom-only stash of chocolate safe from little fingers. Some days our survival depended upon it. If momma didn't have chocolate to smooth over the rough spots, their lives could be in danger.

Don't judge. We've all been there.

Not only did I hide my chocolate stash from my children, I also hid to consume it. If I was down to the last Reese's Peanut Butter Cup and didn't want to cut it into three equal pieces, I'd go in another room to eat it.

It seldom worked.

My house was small, the walls were thin, and my children's hearing was sharp. They could hear a wrapper crackle three rooms away. If you're a Reese's Peanut Butter Cup lover, you know you have to peel off two wrappers before you can pop that luscious piece of candy into your mouth. Even a well-timed cough to cover the sound of the crinkle wasn't enough to mask the sound from my kids. Why, oh why, hasn't someone marketed a silent candy wrapper? They could call it Our Secret and make millions.

Another reason I couldn't hide my chocolate was because my daughters could smell it a mile away. With noses like bears hunting honey, they'd sniff the air and home in on me. Even if I closed my mouth and breathed only through my nose, somehow the scent escaped.

"I smell chocolate!" one would pronounce, eyeing me suspiciously.

I'd scrunch my eyebrows together, sniff the air, and say through barely-opened lips, "Chocolate? I don't smell any chocolate."

Apparently enough scent molecules escaped with those six words to give them the evidence they needed. I was busted every time. Why did I even *try* to hide something as amazing as chocolate?

I thought of my chocolate-hiding days when I read the seventh chapter of Mark.

Jesus's fame was spreading. His reputation to heal, cast out demons, and change lives was becoming more widely known. Whenever He entered a city, people thronged to catch a glimpse of Him. Many laid their sick on the road, hoping their loved ones would be healed if His shadow touched them.

In Mark 6, the crowds were so unrelenting, and the disciples so tired, that Jesus sent them away to a desert place to rest. Even that didn't work. Word quickly spread that He was in the area. Before long, they were surrounded again. Jesus ministered until late at night, healing, comforting, and teaching.

One day He went to the region of Tyre. "He entered a house and did not want anyone to know it" (Mark 7:24). Please, no crowds.

However, "He could not keep his presence a secret."

Similar to my chocolate (only a billion times more), Jesus was compelling. Life-changing. Transformational. Yet often we try to keep him hidden away, like the eccentric aunt who endangered our cool factor in high school.

Other times we try to compartmentalize Jesus. We brag on Him in church, but avoid talking about Him at work. We tell our Christian friends what He's doing in our lives, but fail to mention Him to others who might not understand. We keep the sweetness of Christ tucked into our secret closets instead of sharing Him with those who need Him most.

If Jesus is real in your life, He cannot (and should not) be hidden. If you've been enjoying Him in secret, maybe it's time to unwrap Him so everyone can see. Share Him with those around you. Although I felt like I needed chocolate to survive the early days of motherhood, the reality is that we all truly need Jesus. There are people in your life who desperately need you to stop keeping His presence a secret. Unlike the temporary elixir of chocolate, Jesus's transforming power can make an eternal difference.

Uncommon Thought
The magnificence of Jesus's power and presence can't be minimized or tucked into a corner.

Unusual Faith
Pray and ask God to show you with whom you can unwrap and share Jesus today. Trust Him to give you the compassion and courage you need to speak up.

Read Mark 7:24–37.

Thinking about Our Departure

About eight days after Jesus said this, he took Peter, John
and James with him and went up onto a mountain to pray.
As he was praying, the appearance of his face changed,
and his clothes became as bright as a flash of lightning.
Two men, Moses and Elijah, appeared in glorious splendor,
talking with Jesus. They spoke about his departure, which
he was about to bring to fulfillment at Jerusalem.

LUKE 9:28–31

Cancer is cruel. So are other chronic, wasting diseases that slowly suck the life out of a mind or body. The physical and emotional roller-coaster rides that accompany a long illness can be one of the most heartbreaking experiences a family can endure.

During my mother-in-law's last days, however, I discovered that chronic conditions also bring certain gifts. Instead of arriving wrapped in pretty paper and tied with bows, they often come dressed in hospital gowns and tied with IV tubing. But they are gifts, nonetheless.

Terminal illness removes the suddenness that often comes with death and gives people the time and opportunity to be intentional about their last days. When people know they have a condition that could end their life, they usually become more deliberate. They dust off their bucket list, initiate hard conversations, or rid their lives of activities that don't really matter.

My mother-in-law, reigning over the final days of her life from a hospital bed, made very deliberate choices about how she spent each day. Highest on her priority list were people and relationships. Because she knew there was a good chance she wouldn't recover, she wanted to be sure she left this world with no regrets.

We don't normally like to talk, or even think about, our own departure from this world, but it's biblical. Jesus talked often about His death. We see a snippet of one of these conversations in the book of Luke:

> About eight days after Jesus said this, he took Peter, John and
> James with him and went up onto a mountain to pray. As he
> was praying, the appearance of his face changed, and his clothes
> became as bright as a flash of lightning. Two men, Moses and
> Elijah, appeared in glorious splendor, talking with Jesus. *They
> spoke about his departure*, which he was about to bring to fulfill-
> ment at Jerusalem. (Luke 9:28–31, emphasis mine)

I can't imagine what the conversation about Jesus's impending torture, crucifixion, and death might have included, but it made a profound impact on his disciples. Especially Peter. Emulating his Savior, he recorded his own departure conversation years later. Listen to 2 Peter 1:13–18:

> I think it is right to refresh your memory as long as I live in the
> tent of this body, because I know that I will soon put it aside,
> as our Lord Jesus Christ has made clear to me. And I will make

every effort to see that after my departure you will always be
able to remember these things.

What did Peter want others to remember after his departure? The
truth about Jesus. As Peter faced his impending death, he wanted to
ensure that those around him remained strong in the faith. This is
why he told and retold the story of hearing God's voice on the Mount
of Transfiguration, affirming that Jesus was, indeed, the Son of God.
Listen:

> We did not follow cleverly devised stories when we told you
> about the coming of our Lord Jesus Christ in power, but we
> were eyewitnesses of his majesty. He received honor and glory
> from God the Father when the voice came to him from the
> Majestic Glory, saying, "This is my Son, whom I love; with him
> I am well pleased." We ourselves heard this voice that came
> from heaven when we were with him on the sacred mountain.

During my mother-in-law's final hospital stay, she requested visits
from family members and friends. Some couldn't come in person,
so she called them. Although she had, in the past, feared her own
mortality, she demonstrated what my friend Ken Wingate calls "dying
grace."

"I'm not afraid to die," she told everyone who would listen, "because Jesus is my Savior." She talked more about faith in those last
days than she ever had. As the time of her departure grew near, her
faith and peace grew stronger.

Not all of us will have the *benefit* of an extended illness prior to
our departure. If we, like Peter and my mother-in-law, want to be sure

we'll have no regrets when that day comes, we must begin sowing the seeds of faith in those around us now. In this way, when we take our final breath, we'll know we've used our time well. And, Lord willing, we'll bring a long line of spiritual children with us.

Uncommon Thought

We never know when our lives will end. Whether we die today or in fifty years, living every day conscious of our own mortality can help us finish well, with no regrets.

Unusual Faith

If you knew you were going to die soon, with whom would you want to share your faith? Ask God for an opportunity to talk with them soon. When the chance comes, be bold and winsome.

Read Luke 9:28–36.

The Hardest Mission Field of All

Andrew, Simon Peter's brother, was one of the two who heard what John had said and who had followed Jesus. The first thing Andrew did was to find his brother Simon and tell him, "We have found the Messiah" (that is, the Christ).

JOHN 1:40–41

My friend MacKenzie accepted Christ as her Savior at age twenty-one. Almost immediately she became concerned about the spiritual condition of her five brothers, her mother, and her father. If the Bible were true, then they, too, needed a relationship with Christ. Where they would spend eternity weighed on her mind. As she grew in her faith and experienced joy, peace, and purpose, she desperately wanted her family members to experience these blessings too.

Thus began her "crusade." In her early years as a Christian, she had what the Bible calls zeal without knowledge. She passionately witnessed to her family, telling them often there was a heaven to gain and a hell to avoid. Sometimes she argued. Other times she pleaded. She posted notes with Bible verses on them in prominent places throughout the house. She shared her newfound knowledge with enthusiasm, but not always tact.

Her words bounced off her family like ping-pong balls. The faster and more furiously she pelted them, the quicker they batted them away. They mocked her faith, called her names, and patronized her. After several years of no success and increasing resistance, she grew discouraged.

In John 1 we meet Andrew. One of John the Baptist's followers, Andrew heard John identify Jesus as the Messiah, calling Him "the Lamb of God" (v. 29). He transferred his allegiance to Jesus and followed Him.

Just as my friend MacKenzie had done, Andrew wanted to share his newfound knowledge and faith with his family. In John 1:41 we read, "The first thing Andrew did was to find his brother Simon and tell him, 'We have found the Messiah' (that is, the Christ)."

Andrew's brother was more spiritually minded than MacKenzie's. Scripture tells us Simon Peter believed and followed Christ. After Christ's death and resurrection, Peter became a dynamic evangelist and church leader.

In the years since MacKenzie became a Christian, she's learned a few things about witnessing. Discouraged by her family's negative response, she prayed and asked God how to approach them. For a while she refrained from sharing spiritual things, only mentioning faith when it came up naturally.

Gradually a plan developed. She set out to win her family to Christ by showing them what true faith looks like. Here's her threefold plan:

1. *Show them how much I love them.* Although love had motivated MacKenzie's overzealous witness, it didn't come across that way to her family. Now she works hard to show love in tangible ways. She extends hospitality and remembers birthdays and special occasions with cards and gifts. She asks

how she can pray for them. When her stepfather was diagnosed with cancer, she drove from two states away to visit, read to him, cook special meals, and serve him however she could. She did her best to demonstrate Christ's love.

2. *Approach them with humility and grace.* Sometimes Christians unintentionally project an air of superiority toward unbelievers. If a person feels judged or demeaned, they'll resist our message. Once MacKenzie realized that if it hadn't been for God's grace toward her, she'd still be as lost as her family members, her attitude changed. She became more humble. She learned that she couldn't expect a person who doesn't have a relationship with Christ to act like a Christian. They don't have the Holy Spirit inside them to guide their actions. This insight doesn't mean she accepts everything they do and never speaks up for what's right. Instead she speaks "truth in love."

3. *Ask God for natural opportunities to share. Then be ready.* First Peter 3:15–16 reminds us, "Always be prepared to give an answer to everyone who asks you to give the reason for the hope that you have. But do this with gentleness and respect, keeping a clear conscience, so that those who speak maliciously against your good behavior in Christ may be ashamed of their slander."

Whenever she visited her family, MacKenzie prayed and asked God to give her opportunities to share her faith. Because her life was centered around Christ, she found it natural to share experiences, answered prayers, and examples of how God was working in her life. Instead of "preaching," she told winsome personal stories.

MacKenzie's been a Christian for more than thirty years and is just beginning to see the spiritual fruit of her labors. Her loving care toward her stepfather opened the door for a spiritual conversation during his last hospitalization. Three days before he died, she shared the gospel with him, and he prayed to receive Christ. One of her cousins is now walking with the Lord. Some family members seem further away than ever, but others, like her mother, are softening toward spiritual things. Her brothers still give her a hard time, but their pushback is usually more playful than hostile.

Sometimes she grows weary, but, like Simon Peter's brother, Andrew, she's committed to faithfully witness to her family for as long as it takes in the hope that some will come to faith.

Uncommon Thought
Faithful love and a winsome witness are the twin keys that can unlock even the hardest heart.

Unusual Faith
Think about your family members who don't yet have a relationship with Christ. Pray and ask God to show you specific ways you can demonstrate love toward them. Ask Him to give you natural opportunities to share your faith. Then be brave and share your hope with them.

Read John 1:29–51.

Evangelism's Secret Weapon

The Lord opened her heart to respond to Paul's message.

ACTS 16:14

I became a Christian when I was eighteen years old. My conversion was a surprise, really, because prior to that day, if I'd had to check a survey box, I'd have chosen *Christian*. I'd walked the aisle of a church, knelt at the altar, and prayed the sinner's prayer. It doesn't get any more Christian than that.

But in spite of that prayer, nothing in my life changed. I could sin and it didn't bother me. I went to church to hang out with my friends, not to worship God. I had no desire to read my Bible, or pray, or share my faith. My name was on the Sunday school roster, but I was as lost as a farm girl in Brooklyn.

Then one day something peculiar happened. All the Scripture I'd been listening to from the back row of the church began working on my heart. I started to see my sin for what it was—an offense against a holy God. I grew increasingly uncomfortable. My flippant disregard for truth and purity made me more and more squirmy. Despite having a full-tuition scholarship to the college of my choice, a steady boy-friend, and a bright future, I became restless, anxious, and discontent.

The book of Acts tells the story of a woman a lot like me. Her name was Lydia, and she, too, was living the good life. She enjoyed professional success, was well-respected in the community, and met regularly with religious people.

But she hadn't surrendered her life to Jesus. Like me, she was doing the right things on the outside, but something was missing on the inside. She lacked joy, peace, and holiness.

Then the apostle Paul told her about Jesus, and "the Lord opened her heart to respond to Paul's message" (Acts 16:14). She surrendered control of her life to God and was baptized. Her family witnessed her dramatic transformation and also came to faith in Christ.

Hungry for more of the life-changing truth Paul and Timothy shared, she begged them to remain as guests in her home. Later she opened her home for Paul and Silas to meet with other believers, and the church in Philippi was born. Paul's letter to the Philippians was written to this church, and it all began when God opened Lydia's heart to believe.

Scripture teaches that no one comes to Jesus unless the Father draws him (John 6:65). The spiritually dead cannot receive the truth. God must crack the hard shell of resistance that covers their hearts and breathe life into their souls.

Knowing this gives us a secret weapon for evangelizing—prayer.

After I trusted Christ as my Savior, I felt an overwhelming desire to share my newfound faith with those closest to me. I wanted them to experience the same joy I felt. I also feared for them, understanding for the first time that if they died without trusting Christ, they'd spend eternity separated from God. The weight of spiritual responsibility weighed heavy on my heart.

Because talking about spiritual things with those closest to us is scary, we must bathe every conversation in prayer. When we do, we remind ourselves that it isn't our cleverly crafted speeches or sophisticated arguments that will bring about transformation; it's the work of the Holy Spirit. If you're burdened for a lost friend or loved one, here are three ways you can pray:

1. Ask God to orchestrate the circumstances of their lives to help them realize their need for Him.
2. Pray for God to give you the ability to see how He's working in their life and the wisdom to know how to come alongside Him.
3. Ask God to soften their heart to receive your words.

When we pray for our lost loved ones, we acknowledge that true conversion is a work of the Holy Spirit. Knowing this frees us to share our faith with confidence, trusting that God will go ahead of us into the conversation.

If you have friends or loved ones who haven't yet placed their faith in Christ, witnessing is important, but praying is equally important. And when you pray, remember to ask God to open their hearts to respond, just like He did with mine and Lydia's.

Uncommon Thought
Unless God opens a person's heart, the message of the gospel falls on deaf ears.

Unusual Faith
Think of the people you'd most like to see come to faith in Christ. Pray daily, asking God to open their hearts to believe. Then look for opportunities to share your faith with them.

Read Acts 16:12–15.

How to Live When Every Day Is Saturday

> We know that our old self was crucified with him so
> that the body ruled by sin might be done away with,
> that we should no longer be slaves to sin—because
> anyone who has died has been set free from sin.
>
> ROMANS 6:6–7

The first Good Friday wasn't very good. In fact, it's the ultimate horror show of the Bible.

Think about it. The story has all the necessary elements of a nightmare thriller. It begins with a protagonist who brings hope and healing to a downtrodden people. He's the friend of sinners who champions the cause of the poor, the sick, and the oppressed. He challenges the twin demagogues of religion and government and vanquishes them with His wisdom and intellect. He's witty, quick-thinking, and compassionate. And He loves and cares for His mother. Can a hero get any better than that?

All goes well until a surprise plot twist finds Him betrayed by one of His closest confidants, abandoned by His friends, and arrested by corrupt, power-hungry men. The dark villain and mastermind of this fiendish plot, Satan himself, cackles with glee as they nail His shredded body to a cross. And then He dies.

Not the happy ending everyone expected. Least of all His disciples.

If Good Friday is the horror show of the Bible, then Resurrection Sunday is the ultimate feel-good movie. The hero kicks the teeth out of death's ravenous mouth, delivers the antidote for sin, and paves the way for all who believe to live forever with Him in the wonderland of heaven.

He rewards the faithful and punishes the wicked. His triumph resounds with all the bells and whistles heaven can muster: an earthquake, angels, and a vanishing body. No longer bound by the frailty of human flesh, the conquering hero amazes His followers with the ability to read minds, appear and disappear, and walk through locked doors.

If we're believers, we're united with Christ in His death and resurrection. We died with Him on Good Friday. We surrendered our right to self-government and independence. We threw in our lot with Jesus and turned our back on the person we used to be, the person who lived for herself. We irrevocably declared our desire to surrender, submit, and be sanctified.

"We know that our old self was crucified with him so that the body ruled by sin might be done away with, that we should no longer be slaves to sin—because anyone who has died has been set free from sin" (Romans 6:6–7).

And we'll one day live and reign with Him in heaven forever. That's Resurrection Sunday.

We'll shed our slimy scales of sinful flesh and don the robes of righteousness Christ has prepared for us. We'll no longer be hindered by the frailties of our human bodies. No more sickness, pain, sorrow, or death. We'll receive rewards for the deeds we did for Christ alone— gold, silver, and precious stones—and lay them at His feet. Faith will become sight, and all will be made right.

But stuck in the middle of Good Friday and Resurrection Sunday is Saturday. The awful in-between. The no-man's-land between faith and sight. This is where we're living now. We believe Christ died, was buried, and rose again, but we have yet to see Him. We spend our time, money, and energy to further the kingdom He promised, but few have seen it this side of the veil. We pray to a Savior we cannot see because we believe He can see us. We wait in confident expectation to receive the redemption of our bodies and our souls. But our faith isn't sight on Saturday.

> For the creation was subjected to frustration, not by its own choice, but by the will of the one who subjected it, in hope that the creation itself will be liberated from its bondage to decay and brought into the freedom and glory of the children of God. . . . Not only so, but we ourselves, who have the firstfruits of the Spirit, groan inwardly as we wait eagerly for our adoption to sonship, the redemption of our bodies. For in this hope we were saved. But hope that is seen is no hope at all. Who hopes for what they already have? But if we hope for what we do not yet have, we wait for it patiently. (Romans 8:20–21, 23–25)

As you live in between Good Friday and Resurrection Sunday, don't lose heart. It's Saturday, but Sunday's coming. And Resurrection Sunday is every bit as real as Good Friday. You can bet your life on it.

Uncommon Thought

After dying with Christ in salvation and before reigning with Christ through resurrection, we live in between faith and sight.

Unusual Faith

Because we are entrenched in the all-too-earthly, day-to-day events of this world, it's easy to forget that what we see isn't all that exists. Take a few minutes to imagine what it will be like when you go to heaven. Close your eyes and picture what you will see, hear, smell, taste, and touch. Lastly, picture the moment when you see Jesus.

Read Romans 8:18–25.

Is Guilt Silencing You?

I am the least of the apostles and do not
even deserve to be called an apostle,
because I persecuted the church of God.

1 CORINTHIANS 15:9

After Jesus, biblical historians agree that the apostle Paul is probably the greatest man who ever lived. Yet he said of himself, "I am the least of the apostles and do not even deserve to be called an apostle, because I persecuted the church of God" (1 Corinthians 15:9).

Paul (also called Saul) was an up-and-coming wonder boy. A Hebrew of Hebrews, he advanced in Judaism beyond many of his peers and was extremely zealous for the traditions of his fathers.

He had all the training and pedigree he needed. Poised to become a leader of the Pharisees, he might even have succeeded the most esteemed teacher.

In his own words, he was obsessed—obsessed with this sect called the Way and their now-dead leader, Jesus Christ. Like many of his countrymen, Saul held firmly to the Jewish expectation that the Messiah would come not as a suffering servant but as a conquering hero. He would free His people from the heavy yoke of Roman rule and reestablish them as world leaders.

Saul believed it—until that day on the road to Damascus.

Blinded by a light so bright it seared his eyes and thrust him into darkness, Saul heard God's voice ask a horrifying question: "Saul, why do you persecute me?"

"Who are you, Lord?" he asked.

And then the terrifying answer: "I am Jesus, whom you are persecuting" (Acts 9:5).

Although shrouded in physical darkness, for the first time, Saul could see.

He could see that Jesus was the promised Messiah. That the stories of His death and resurrection were true. That there was peace, and hope, and eternal life available for those who would trust in Christ as Savior.

And that he had missed it all.

He had spurned Christ as He walked the streets of Jerusalem. He had dedicated his life to the institution that manipulated Jesus's death. He had cheered on those who had stoned the church's first martyr. He had arrested men, women, and even children simply for believing in Jesus.

These truths came crashing down on Saul the Pharisee.

For days he sat in darkness, eating and drinking nothing, wrestling with the depth of his blindness, the weight of his actions, and the burden of his guilt.

Imagine how it felt to sit alone with this horrifying realization on his conscience.

And then, an even greater sorrow: discovering that he, a devout Jew living zealously for the kingdom, had missed the Messiah.

Scripture tells us Saul placed his faith in Christ during that sight-blinding, eye-opening Damascus Road experience, yet God allowed him to remain in darkness for days before God summoned a believing Jew named Ananias to come to his aid.

Perhaps Saul needed this time to humbly accept the healing touch of a disciple he had sought to destroy. The same hands he had hoped to see chained to a prison wall touched his eyes and made him see.

"Brother Saul," Ananias said. "Receive your sight."

Brother Saul.

Instantly Saul's vision returned. Scales fell from his eyes, and he looked deep into the face of a man he had come to persecute.

"The God of our ancestors has chosen you to know his will and to see the Righteous One and to hear words from his mouth," Ananias said. "You will be his witness to all people of what you have seen and heard."

Ananias knew Saul's past. He was familiar with the rap sheet of heinous acts he had committed. He also knew that guilt and shame could cripple Saul and render him useless for the cause of Christ. So he gave Saul his marching orders.

"And now what are you waiting for? Get up, be baptized and wash your sins away, calling on his name" (Acts 22:14–16).

Saul would later write, "But by the grace of God I am what I am, and his grace to me was not without effect" (1 Corinthians 15:10).

Paul never forgot how he persecuted the church of Christ. He never made excuses or tried to hide his behavior. He was open and honest about who he was, but he didn't stay there. He planted his spiritual feet squarely on the grace of God and marched forward.

Instead of allowing his guilt and shame to defeat him and render him powerless for the kingdom, he leveraged it. Every time he shared his story, he testified that no one is too far gone for God to save them, and no one is too imperfect for God to use them.

"You think you're bad?" I can hear him say. "Let me tell you what I did . . . And then let me tell you what Jesus has done in my life."

Uncommon Thought

Oftentimes we allow the guilt and shame of our mistakes to silence us. Instead, like Paul, we can use our story to demonstrate how mightily God can transform a person who is humble and repentant.

Unusual Faith

Consider the parts of your life that fill you with regret and shame. If you haven't already done so, confess these sins to God and ask Him to forgive you. Thank Him for granting His forgiveness, removing the guilt of your past, and making you a new person. Ask Him to give you the opportunity (with prayerful discretion) to share your story with someone who doesn't know Christ or someone who's feeling inadequate to serve Him.

If you're struggling with present failures and inadequacies and the feelings of defeat that accompany them, realize that God's blanket of grace and forgiveness extends to you as well. Accept, like Paul did, that Christ's righteousness covers all our sins and shortcomings—past, present, and future. Then walk in the victory Christ secured for you on the cross.

Read 1 Corinthians 15:3–10.

2 CORINTHIANS

True Repentance

> See what this godly sorrow has produced in you: what
> earnestness, what eagerness to clear yourselves, what
> indignation, what alarm, what longing, what concern,
> what readiness to see justice done. At every point you
> have proved yourselves to be innocent in this matter.
>
> 2 CORINTHIANS 7:11

When the police officer called to tell our pastor he'd caught the person who broke into our church, he shared disturbing news.

"Your thief is sixteen years old," the officer said. "This is his second offense. Do you want to prosecute?"

"I'd like to talk with him before I decide," our pastor said.

When they met the following day, the teen slouched in a chair in the pastor's office, legs splayed and arms crossed, refusing to make eye contact.

"Son," our pastor said, "did you break into my church?"

"Yup."

"And did you steal a guitar, a speaker, and a computer?"

"Yup."

"Why?"

"'Cause I wanted to, that's why," he said defiantly.

"I suspect you know that stealing is wrong. You've sinned against our church, and you've sinned against God. Is there anything you'd like to say to me about what you did?"

"Nope."

"Then this conversation is over." Turning to the officer that stood nearby, he said four sad words. "I'd like to prosecute."

Our pastor had hoped to offer forgiveness that day. If the young man had acknowledged his sin and repented, he planned to work with him, offering the chance for restitution and rehabilitation. Without a repentant heart, however, our pastor knew he had nothing to work with.

In the fifth chapter of 1 Corinthians, Paul addresses a very different sin than breaking and entering, yet at the heart of both offenses is the matter of true repentance. Members of the church in Corinth were engaging in sexual immorality. And not just your garden variety of immorality, but sexual immorality "of a kind that even pagans do not tolerate" (v. 1).

The MacArthur Daily Bible adds this commentary: "This sin was so vile that even the church's pagan neighbors were doubtless scandalized by it."[10] Now if the pagans are scandalized by it, you know it's bad. Sadly, neither the sinning members nor the church took the sin seriously.

With apostolic authority, Paul challenged the offending members and the church. And he chronicles the happy ending in 2 Corinthians 7—all those involved repented and were restored. Unlike the young man who broke into our church, the members of the Corinthian church displayed characteristics of true repentance. Let's look at a few of them, as described in verse 11.

Godly sorrow. Because repentance, as MacArthur defines it, "refers to the desire to turn from one's sin and restore one's relationship with God," godly sorrow is a necessary component. Different from regret, which often focuses on wishing we hadn't sinned because we got in trouble, godly sorrow springs from the conviction of the Holy Spirit that our sin has offended God himself.

Earnestness. The immediate desire to eagerly pursue righteous living.

Eagerness to clear oneself. Not to be confused with trying to avoid punishment, this refers to the repentant sinner's yearning to regain their godly reputation, earn back the spiritual trust they've lost, and no longer shame the name of Christ.

Indignation. In contrast to loving the sin they've committed, those who genuinely repent feel anger at the lies of the world, the flesh, and the devil that enticed them to sin.

Alarm. Fear is appropriate when one has sinned grievously against God. As Isaiah experienced when he saw God in all His glory, we should be frightened to stand before God with sin in our lives. Those who haven't called upon Christ for salvation are one breath away from spending eternity in hell. Those who have a relationship with Christ risk God's discipline. Either prospect should invoke fear.

Longing. Once we've restored our relationship with God through confession and repentance, we must then work to restore the relationships with others that we've damaged by our sin. Longing describes a passion to do whatever it takes to make things right.

Concern. Concern is the dynamic energy that commits itself to maintaining purity and warning others about sin's effects. Some versions of the Bible translate this word *zeal.* As a testimony of God's ability to bring beauty from ashes, sometimes those most entangled in a particular sin become the greatest champions against it.

A readiness to see justice done. No longer committed to protecting themselves from the penalty of their actions, repentant sinners desire justice regarding their sin, no matter what it costs them. The dishonest tax collector, Zacchaeus, in Luke 19, is a beautiful example of this. When he placed his faith in Christ, he confessed his sin and expressed his desire to "pay back four times" what he had wrongfully taken.

For years after the church break-in, our pastor's heart ached for the young man who so defiantly spurned his willingness to forgive. He prayed often that experiencing the consequences of his actions would bring the young man to a place of genuine repentance. Then true change could occur.

Uncommon Thought

To be true and life-changing, repentance requires us to confess and forsake our sin and call upon God to help us banish it from our lives forever.

Unusual Faith

Do you tend to magnify others' offenses and minimize your own? What difference do you think it would make to your relationships if you applied the principles of true repentance as found in 2 Corinthians 7? Commit today, the next time you sin against someone, to biblically repent.

Read 2 Corinthians 7:8–11.

Always Wanted

God, who set me apart from my mother's
womb and called me by his grace.

GALATIANS 1:15

I always knew my parents wanted me. From my earliest existence, I
was welcomed, celebrated (maybe too much), and loved. Not because
I was the firstborn, but because I was the second.

My brother, Robert, was born just eighteen months prior to me.
He lived only three days. Complications from a challenging delivery
took him from my parents before they even had a chance to hold him.
My mother was only eighteen years old.

In time God blessed them with another baby—me. Halfway
through Mom's pregnancy, her doctor discovered a cyst on her ovary.
It blocked the birth canal and took up much-needed space in her
abdomen.

Without surgery, my growth and development would be hindered,
and my mother would be unable to deliver me. But with the surgery
came the risk that I could be born deaf, blind, or both. The procedure
could also trigger early labor. In the sixties, babies born three months
prematurely had little or no chance of survival.

Imagine what it would be like to be nineteen years old, mourning the loss of your first child, and fearing for the life of your second. My mom went to sleep in the operating room. My dad chain-smoked in the waiting room. "We didn't know if you'd make it," he told me years later. "I don't know how we'd have borne it if you hadn't."

As you already know, I survived. I arrived right on schedule three months later, neither blind nor deaf. As you can imagine, my parents celebrated my birth as a grand and glorious gift from God.

Unlike me, not everyone has the privilege of being wanted by their parents. Some don't even know their parents. Many were born into impoverished, dysfunctional, or turbulent homes and families. Others were "unplanned" or "unwanted." Some were celebrated, but later, when the winds of circumstance changed, they became a burden.

Whether we were wanted or unwanted by the people in our lives, the apostle Paul's words to the church in Galatia speak truth: "God, who set me apart from my mother's womb and called me by his grace."

What does it mean, for Paul and for us, to be set apart from our mother's womb and called by God's grace? Here are three truths to consider:

1. *Your birth was not an accident or a mistake.* Psalm 139:15–16 reads, "My frame was not hidden from you when I was made in the secret place, when I was woven together. . . . Your eyes saw my unformed body; all the days ordained for me were written in your book before one of them came to be."

2. *You were set apart for a purpose.* Paul's purpose was to preach Christ to the Gentiles, yet he didn't start out that way.

Instead, he persecuted the church of Christ, jailing and killing sincere believers. But instead of disqualifying him from the purpose for which God had set him apart, his tragic early years added weight to his testimony that Christ came into the world to save sinners, of whom he was the worst.

Our purpose may be something less grandiose than evangelizing half of the known world, but it is significant, nonetheless. We may never understand how our life impacts others, but we can rest assured, God will use us for His glory.

3. *Our encounter with God wasn't by chance.* On the contrary, before the foundations of the world were formed, God ordered our days. Through a divine work of grace, He revealed himself to you (perhaps He's doing this right now) and called you to himself. No one comes to Jesus, the Bible says, unless God the Father draws him. What a thought. God invites imperfect people like us to have a relationship with Him—the almighty God of the universe.

I don't know your background. You may have read my story and wished it were yours (minus the part about my brother). Maybe you've always longed to be treasured and loved. If you've spent most of your life feeling more like a burden and less like a blessing, consider this: On the day you were born, God welcomed you, celebrated you, and loved you. He set you apart for His glory and good pleasure. He's inviting you, by His grace, to walk with Him all the days of your life.

Uncommon Thought

Whether or not you were wanted by your mother, father, or other significant person in your life, God the Father has always wanted you.

Unusual Faith

Think back over your life. Have you ever felt unwanted? Have you doubted your value or questioned if your life has a purpose? Instead of allowing the circumstances of your birth or the opinions of others to define you, embrace the truth of Galatians 1. You have been set apart by God and called for His glory. Tuck this truth deep into your soul and embrace it. When other people's words or the voices in your head contradict what you know to be true, personalize and quote this verse aloud. "God set me apart from my mother's womb and called me by his grace."

Read Galatians 1:15–24.

Is It Worth Fighting Over?

Be completely humble and gentle; be patient, bearing
with one another in love. Make every effort to keep
the unity of the Spirit through the bond of peace.

EPHESIANS 4:2–3

Our country is one big argument. People from different political parties, ideologies, races, perspectives, and walks of life disagree with each other and take offense at any little thing. We agree that our country would be stronger, happier, and more peaceful if we were unified, yet we have no idea how to make it happen.

Sadly, the church is often no different. The universal body of Christ argues over denominational differences, nonvital points of theology, and methodology. Local churches disagree on issues that are a matter of preference, personality, and style. Minor issues become major ones, and before we know it, a church is divided, and Satan cheers.

Yet sometimes disagreement is necessary. Some issues *are* worth contending for, and to compromise would harm the cause of Christ and damage the church. How can we tell the difference?

We can tell by asking this question: Is the root of our disagreement preference, sin, or conviction? Most conflicts arise because of one of these three reasons.

Preference

One winner of the "Who Can Start a Fight Quicker?" award is preference. Most of the arguments in my life have been based on preference. When I examine the debris field after an explosion, I usually discover that we fought because one of us wanted something done the way we preferred it. Each of us *knew* our preference was the best, and we weren't willing to consider that the other's opinion might have merit.

Think about the arguments that occur in your life. Pizza or Chinese? Vegan or carnivore? Spender or saver? Clean or messy? Analyze the shrapnel after the bomb blast, and you'll usually find the conflict covered in preference dust.

In the church, preference is also often the root of disagreement. One prefers praise music and the other prefers hymns. Some prefer to hold VBS in the evening, and others prefer the morning. Neither is fundamentally wrong, just different.

In cases like these, the Lord instructs us through the apostle Paul to be humble and gentle about our opinions, making every effort to preserve unity. We should state our preference, but if the vote doesn't go our way, we must yield gracefully. I've often found when I yield my preference to someone else's for unity's sake (or at least don't bludgeon them with it), it ceases to be as important. Whatever the decision, it's okay. I've put someone else ahead of me, and this honors God. God remains sovereign, even if the winning choice isn't the best.

Sin

Other disagreements are caused by sin. We're selfish, and it's our way or the highway. Or maybe we manipulate circumstances in our favor and for our benefit, with little regard for anyone else. Other times, we're not even this subtle. We want the best for ourselves, and we'll do whatever it takes to get it, even if it means doing something dishonest or deceitful.

Unfortunately, selfishness also happens in the church. Because the church is made up of sinful people, we bring our dual natures with us into God's house and cause all kinds of trouble. Jealousy, greed, gossip, and pride are just a few sins that can damage the church and the cause of Christ.

When disagreements occur in the church because of sin, we must deal with them with an eye toward repentance and restoration. If sin is at the root of a disagreement, we must humbly and lovingly address the issue. We must treat others the way we'd want to be treated, without overlooking or winking at sin. Matthew 18:15–20 gives a God-honoring, time-tested way to resolve conflict.

Convictions

A third reason for conflict is disagreement related to our convictions. A conviction is a firmly held belief. A biblical conviction is a belief derived from and based on a commitment to Scripture.

People sometimes confuse preference with conviction, especially in the church, so let me give you a couple of examples: I prefer using the Holman Christian Standard Bible, but if I visited a church that preached from the NIV or the King James Version, I'd willingly participate. If, however, the church taught from the Book of Mormon, my conviction that only the Bible is the Word of God wouldn't allow me to participate.

I prefer to attend services in a church building, but if someone invited me to attend a worship service on the beach, I'd go. As long as the doctrine is sound, it shouldn't matter where we worship. If, however, the government forbade me to worship Jesus at all, my conviction to worship God would mean I'd have to disobey the law and worship God despite the threat of punishment.

When Paul admonishes us in Galatians to make every effort to preserve the unity of the Spirit, he means yielding our preferences and dealing with our sin. He doesn't tell us to maintain unity by compromising our convictions.

Because convictions are rooted in a thorough understanding of God's Word and a commitment to uphold it, we must defend them, even if we cause "disunity." If a church, movement, or denomination promotes doctrine that contradicts the Bible, we must separate from them.

In many situations, God calls us to gently yield our preferences and humbly confess our sin in an attempt to live in harmony with our Christian brothers and sisters. But when someone attacks, distorts, or misrepresents the truths of the Word of God, it's time to stand up and speak up. Convictions based on God's Word are worth fighting for.

Uncommon Thought
God, through Paul, didn't call for unity at any cost. Sometimes He calls us to speak up.

Unusual Faith
Think back on your most recent conflict and ask yourself, "Is it caused by preference, sin, or conviction?" If you're not sure, ask God

to reveal the root of the matter to you through His Word or the wise counsel of godly believers. Depending on the answer, either yield your preference, confess your sin (or forgive someone else's), or stand on convictions. Trust God to honor your step of faith.

Read Ephesians 4:1–6.

In Life or in Death

I eagerly expect and hope that I will in no way
be ashamed, but will have sufficient courage
so that now as always Christ will be exalted
in my body, whether by life or by death.

PHILIPPIANS 1:20

My thirty-five-year-old Bible study leader, Billy, went to the doctor for headaches and returned with a diagnosis of brain cancer. My friend Sue fell ill one day while visiting her eighty-year-old father. She was stunned when the ER doctor told her she had pancreatic cancer. And the apostle Paul, jailed by a government that tortured and crucified Christians, didn't wonder *if* he was going to die. He wondered when.

I haven't walked the cancer road, nor have I languished in prison awaiting execution. I have pondered the possibility of my own death. A frightening lab result and a one-month wait for diagnostic surgery caused me to wrestle with my mortality.

During that long month, I dug deep and prayed hard. I knew, like Billy, Sue, and Paul, that God doesn't always heal or deliver the way we hope. Sometimes God answers our prayers with a no and allows people to die. It hurts my heart to write these words, because if we're praying for someone we love who's fighting for his or her life, we don't want to acknowledge this possibility. But the apostle Paul knew it was true, and he showed us, by example, how to face a potential death sentence with grace and faith.

In Philippians 1:23–24, he identified the struggle: "I am torn between the two: I desire to depart and be with Christ, which is better by far; but it is more necessary for you that I remain in the body." Paul longed to be with Christ, but accepted his assignment here on earth a little longer. My friends Billy and Sue were comforted by the promise of heaven, yet they were acutely aware of the needs of those they loved here on earth. Billy had a wife and two young sons. Sue helped care for her aging father.

Yet God mysteriously uses Christians in difficult circumstances as powerful witnesses for Christ: "What has happened to me has really served to advance the gospel," Paul says. We can almost see him shake his head in amazement. Not only was the gospel message not hindered by his imprisonment, God used it to bring people to Christ who might otherwise never have heard.

When Billy accepted his cancer as an opportunity to testify to God's sovereignty over his life, his faith was so radiant that people everywhere wanted to hear his story. Our church invited him to speak at a men's ministry event. More than five hundred men attended, including his brother, who didn't know God. After hearing Billy speak, his brother asked Christ to be his Savior. More than anything, he said, he wanted the type of peace, faith, and trust Billy had.

My friend Sue used her CaringBridge site to share the faith lessons she learned during her journey with cancer. She pointed others to God and encouraged them by her example to trust Him even when they didn't understand what He was doing. Because she trusted God and sought to glorify Him regardless of the outcome of her illness, God used her to witness to hundreds of people she encountered.

Paul's goal, which Billy and Sue shared, can be ours as well, no matter what challenge we face: "I eagerly expect and hope that I will in no way be ashamed, but will have sufficient courage so that now as always Christ will be exalted in my body, whether by life or by death" (Philippians 1:20).

It's not wrong to pray for God to bring glory to himself by restoring someone to health. My cancer-free biopsy result is one example. As I prayed for a clear report, however, I also asked God to help me trust him regardless of the outcome.

"Whatever happens," Paul says, "conduct yourselves in a manner worthy of the gospel of Christ" (v. 27).

Eighteenth-century theologian Oswald Chambers wrote, "As a saint of God, my attitude toward sorrow and difficulty should not be to ask that they be prevented, but to ask that God protect me so that I may remain what He created me to be, in spite of all my fires of sorrow."[11]

Is death bad? Absolutely. God's original plan for the world didn't include sickness and death. But sin's curse has wrapped its poisonous tentacles around our world causing death and destruction since Adam and Eve sinned in the garden of Eden.

One day, however, God will banish sin, sickness, and death. Until then, we must trust that God allows these things in our lives so we can show Jesus to the world. Whether in life or in death, He calls us to conduct ourselves in a manner worthy of the gospel of Christ. This will point others to Him and bring Him glory.

Because God can use even death to bring glory to himself and advance the gospel, then maybe dying isn't always a bad thing.

Uncommon Thought

It's not wrong to pray for healing. An even greater prayer, however, would be to ask God to give us or our loved ones the grace and faith to exalt Him—whether in life or in death.

Unusual Faith

If you're facing a crisis, health or otherwise, surrender your will to God's. Ask Him to resolve the situation in the way that will bring Him the most glory. Then trust Him.

Read Philippians 1:1–30.

Wrestling in Prayer

Devote yourselves to prayer,
being watchful and thankful.

<small>COLOSSIANS</small> 4:2

One of my hardest days of motherhood was the day my husband and I left our youngest daughter at college. We'd asked God for direction and provision and believed God had directed us to a Christian college two states away. But when move-in day came, the assurance that had guided our decision vanished.

As we sat in the parent orientation, only hours away from saying goodbye, tears filled my eyes. I forced myself to listen to the campus pastor.

"I want you to know that we've been praying for your children since we first knew their names," he said. "This is what we've been praying." He clicked his pointer, and Colossians 1:9–12 filled the screen.

> For this reason, since the day we heard about you, we have not
> stopped praying for you. We continually ask God to fill you with
> the knowledge of his will through all the wisdom and under-
> standing that the Spirit gives, so that you may live a life worthy of

the Lord and please him in every way: bearing fruit in every good work, growing in the knowledge of God, being strengthened with all power according to his glorious might so that you may have great endurance and patience, and giving joyful thanks to the Father, who has qualified you to share in the inheritance of his holy people in the kingdom of light.

When I saw the words on the screen, I lost it.

Tears streamed down my cheeks, but not the tears of grief and fear I'd been suppressing. Instead they were tears of sweet relief.

Why?

Four years earlier, I had read Colossians 4:2: "Devote yourselves to prayer, being watchful and thankful." I read about Epaphras, who was "always wrestling in prayer" for others (4:12). And I read the passage the campus pastor referenced, Colossians 1:9–12. It was chock full of good things to pray for my daughter, so I had prayed those verses. Almost every day for years.

That morning during parent orientation, the Lord used the verses He had led me to pray for my daughter to calm my anxious spirit and give me confidence that my daughter was right where she was supposed to be.

If you're new to prayer, or if you're struggling to master the discipline, here are four simple guidelines from Colossians 4.

Devote yourselves to prayer. To be devoted to something means to be committed—when things go well and when things fall apart. When we feel like it, and when we don't. When we see results, and when nothing seems to change. We devote ourselves to prayer by faith, because God tells us to.

Be watchful and thankful. When we pray, we don't fling requests up to heaven and forget them. Instead, God calls us to pray and watch for answers. And while we sow the seeds of prayer and wait for God to produce a harvest, we soften and till the ground with our expressions of thanksgiving.

It's an awesome privilege to bring our requests before the King of Kings and Lord of Lords and know we'll always have an audience. We can thank Him for responding to our prayers with wisdom and love, believing that His heart seeks only two things: our good and His glory. And finally (this takes mature faith), we thank Him for answering no to some of our prayers, trusting that He knows best.

Wrestle in prayer. "Soul sweat" is how one prayer warrior described it. This type of wrestling involves rolling up our sleeves and interceding until God brings about a breakthrough or He frees us from the burden.

Jesus's disciples came to Him after they unsuccessfully attempted to exorcise a demon. "Why couldn't we drive it out?" they asked.

"This kind can come out only by prayer," Jesus replied (Mark 9:28–29). And He wasn't talking about occasional, half-hearted, wimpy prayers. He was talking about take-your-opponent-to-the-mat-and-hold-him-there kinds of prayers. Epaphras was this kind of spiritual warrior, going to the mat again and again on behalf of God's people and God's kingdom.

Allow the riches of God's Word to fuel and direct your prayers. When we're clueless about what to pray, God's Word provides the template. When we feel betrayed, abandoned, or frightened, the framework of the Psalms can structure our prayers. When we lack insight or inspiration for how to pray for our loved ones, we find direction in the New Testament Epistles.

Because Paul and other inspired writers wrote letters to fellow believers, they often penned blessings and challenges for their beloved brothers and sisters. When I discovered Colossians 1:9–12, I knew I wanted to pray these attributes for my children. As you read your Bible, watch for blessings and character qualities to pray for your loved ones. Underline them, write them on index cards with your loved one's name on them, or copy the verses into your prayer journal.

Many activities compete for our time, but we'll never regret the hours we devote to prayer. While the wrestling is anything but pleasant, as we watch expectantly and with thanksgiving, we'll see God do great and mighty things in response. I, for one, don't want to miss that. How about you?

Uncommon Thought
We invest much of our time and effort on the everyday matters of life, but prayer enables us to impact our world for eternity. Can you think of a better return on our investment?

Unusual Faith
Print or write out Colossians 1:9–12. Post it in a prominent place. Pray the verses daily for a week for someone you love, boldly claiming all the good things God promises on their behalf.

Read Colossians 1:1–12.

1 THESSALONIANS

Reveille and Taps

For the Lord himself will come down from heaven, with a
loud command, with the voice of the archangel and with
the trumpet call of God, and the dead in Christ will rise
first. After that, we who are still alive and are left will be
caught up together with them in the clouds to meet the
Lord in the air. And so we will be with the Lord forever.

1 THESSALONIANS 4:16–17

Every morning at 5:55, bugle fanfare echoes across the quiet streets
of my neighborhood. It's first call, a signal to the troops that morning
has arrived. Five minutes later, reveille sounds. Reveille, which origi-
nates from the French word meaning "wake up," began as a way to
rouse military personnel at dawn. At Fort Jackson, in my home city
of Columbia, South Carolina, reveille also signals the raising of the
American flag.

Trumpet calls are not unique to the United States military. They
go back to the dawn of civilization. When God summoned Moses to
Mount Sinai, He used thunder, lightning, and a trumpet call (Exodus
19:19). Leaders used trumpets made of rams' horns to assemble the
Israelites for holy days, gather troops for battle, and direct battle ma-
neuvers. Buglers traditionally go ahead of troops into battle to provide a rallying point.

During times of war, the bugle is the voice of the general leading the charge. General Daniel Butterfield, a Civil War soldier with the Union army, loved bugle calls. Because troops would often get confused on the battlefield as to which call belonged to their battalion, Butterfield composed his own calls unique to his regiment.

In 1862 he took a French bugle call that had gone out of fashion, rearranged the notes, and repurposed it. He used this call to signal "lights out" to the troops. Within days of introducing it, the call, composed of only twenty-four notes, spread through the ranks. Within weeks, the entire Union army was using "Taps" to signal the close of the day.

At 11:00 p.m., if my windows are open and the night is still, I can hear the soothing sound of "Taps" playing in the darkness.

First Thessalonians 4:16–17 tells of the trumpet blast that will sound at the time of Christ's coming:

> For the Lord himself will come down from heaven, with a loud command, with the voice of the archangel *and with the trumpet call of God*, and the dead in Christ will rise first. After that, we who are still alive and are left will be caught up together with them in the clouds to meet the Lord in the air. And so we will be with the Lord forever. (emphasis mine)

First Corinthians 15:52 gives additional details about this glorious day:

> In a flash, in the twinkling of an eye, at the last trumpet. For *the trumpet will sound*, the dead will be raised imperishable, and we will be changed. (emphasis mine)

Fort Jackson no longer uses a lone bugler to sound the fourteen calls that announce everything from mealtime to lights out. Instead it uses a public address system that residents in nearby neighborhoods like mine have insisted is too loud.

I disagree. I love to hear the bugle calls. I listen for them in the early morning and in the late evening. They remind me that even while I sleep, soldiers are protecting my country and me from harm.

I also listen for the final trumpet call, which helps me remember to live intentionally and make the most of every day. It also reminds me that even while I sleep, God is working out His purposes in the world and preparing me to spend eternity with Him in heaven. If you know Christ as Savior, these truths are yours as well.

In the words of the apostle Paul, "Encourage one another with these words" (1 Thessalonians 4:18).

Uncommon Thought
We can listen for the trumpet call to end all trumpet calls—the one that will announce Christ's return to take His bride, the church, home. Anticipating hearing this call one day reminds us to make the most of every day and live in light of Christ's return.

Unusual Faith
Does the promise of Christ's return fill you with anticipation or with dread? Why? It's easy to become so focused on the things of this world we forget that a better home awaits us. Sometimes we spend so much of our lives building our physical kingdoms that we neglect to invest in eternity. Matthew 6:21 reminds us, "For where your treasure is, there your heart will be also." Invite God to examine your heart and reveal any misplaced priorities or anything or anyone that is preventing you

from wholeheartedly looking forward to His return. List the action steps you need to take to reorder your life and put Him first, and begin to work the plan. Then you can wait with joy and expectation for the sound of the trumpet.

Read 1 Thessalonians 4:1–18.

What Does Your Signature Mean?

> I, Paul, write this greeting in my own hand, which is the distinguishing mark in all my letters. This is how I write.
>
> 2 THESSALONIANS 3:17

My friend Lisa is an encourager. Whenever I'm around her, I come away feeling better about myself. Not given to empty flattery, she somehow always manages to find something affirming to say that lifts my spirits and helps me believe in myself.

My friend Mandy is a prayer warrior. When I ask her to pray about something, I know she'll write it down, date it, and follow up on it. Best of all, I know she'll pray faithfully until I tell her otherwise. When I'm scared or discouraged, I call her, because I know she'll get on her knees on my behalf.

My friend Robin is a witness. She's always sprinkling gospel crumbs into her conversations, hoping to find a hungry soul to feed. Wherever she goes, she looks for someone to invite to our church. One Sunday morning she even invited a young man to church who was jogging in the neighborhood. He stopped at our church to use the restroom, and as he was leaving, true to form, Robin invited him to stay for worship.

Ask anyone who knows Lisa, Mandy, and Robin, and they'll agree that these women have reputations. They're known for their ability to encourage, pray, and invite.

Unfortunately, not everyone has such a stellar reputation. Instead of being known for admirable character traits, they're known for being gossipy, lazy, or hard to get along with. They complain instead of encourage, worry instead of pray, and shy away from talking about spiritual things.

We're all known for something—good, bad, or in between. The apostle Paul, in his second letter to the Thessalonian church, attached his signature to a letter that invites us to consider what reputations we have.

One of the reasons Paul wrote 2 Thessalonians was to reassure early believers who feared they had missed Christ's return. False teachers and prophets said Christ had already come back, and the church had missed Him. Imagine how heartbroken you'd feel if you thought Jesus had come back for His church and left you behind.

To calm their fears, Paul told them what would take place before Jesus returned and the Antichrist came on the historical scene. He encouraged them, telling them to stand firm and continue in the sound doctrine he and others had taught them.

If you were the Thessalonians, would you believe Paul? Of course you would. You'd read his letter with a sigh of relief and a happy heart. You'd tell your fellow church members what he said and dismiss the teaching of those who said otherwise.

Why?

Because Paul had a reputation for trustworthiness and honor. He had demonstrated his commitment to Christ, truth, and sound doctrine. When he signed his name to a letter, you could be sure the contents were legit.

"I, Paul, write this greeting in my own hand, which is the distinguishing mark in all my letters. This is how I write" (2 Thessalonians 3:17).

What do you want to be known for? Some of us are known for qualities associated with our spiritual gifts, like the ability to teach, witness, or give. While it's important to live out these individual gifts, we must also develop a reputation for qualities associated with the fruit of the Spirit: love, joy, peace, patience, kindness, goodness, faithfulness, gentleness, and self-control. Every believer receives these qualities in seed form, but we must cultivate and nurture them so they become consistent parts of our behavior.

I want to be like Paul, and I suspect you do too. I want to have the type of reputation that when people see my name associated with something, they know they can trust it. I may not be as good an encourager as my friend Lisa, or as faithful a prayer warrior as my friend Mandy, or as intentional a witness as my friend Robin, but, like them, I can carve out a reputation I'm not afraid to attach my name to.

What about you? What does your signature mean?

Uncommon Thought
Everyone has a reputation. As a Christian, with God's help, I can build a reputation that accurately reflects Christ.

Unusual Faith
Sit quietly before the Lord. Invite Him to examine your heart and life. Be honest with yourself. Ask: When people think of me, what

character qualities come to mind? What areas would I like to grow in? What behaviors and attitudes do I need to remove from my life? If you're struggling to be objective, ask a trusted friend to answer these questions about you. Write down what the Lord reveals to you. In a prayer of confession and commitment, ask Him to give you opportunities to practice the qualities He wants to develop in you. Invite Him to alert you any time you begin to fall back into negative actions and, instead, choose a God-honoring alternative.

Read 2 Thessalonians 3:1–18.

Taking Hold of True Life

Command those who are rich in this present world . . .
to do good, to be rich in good deeds, and to be generous
and willing to share. In this way they will lay up treasure
for themselves as a firm foundation for the coming age,
so that they may take hold of the life that is truly life.

1 TIMOTHY 6:17–19

I've always breathed a sigh of relief at the verses at the end of the book of 1 Timothy. Like the laminated NO HOMEWORK card my tenth grade English teacher would hand out to those who faithfully completed their assignments, these three verses dangled before me like a biblical free pass. Because Paul wrote verses 17–19 for rich people, and I'm not rich, I knew I could blissfully skip over them.

But then I went to Mexico, where the daily wage was $12 per day. And I visited Spain, where the unemployment rate was 18.2 percent. I learned that 800 million people in the developing world lived on less than $1 a day.[12] And a *New York Times* article revealed, "The typical person in the bottom 5 percent of the American income distribution is still richer than 68 percent of the world's inhabitants."[13]

Suddenly I realized that the verses in 1 Timothy *were* talking to me, because I *am* rich. And so are you. Whether we own a house or live in a government-subsidized apartment, drive a car or ride a bike, dine on steak or eat peanut butter sandwiches, we are rich.

And because we're rich, God calls us "to do good, to be rich in good deeds" (v. 18). The late Reverend E. V. Hill, commenting on God's gracious hand of provision, said, "When God blesses you, he doesn't even have you in mind." His tongue-in-cheek statement makes the point that God often blesses us financially so we can provide for the needs of others through generous and sacrificial giving. As we have been blessed, so we are free (and called) to bless others. Unlike volatile financial riches, the wealth we build by investing in good deeds will accumulate interest for eternity.

We must also "be generous and willing to share" (v. 18). Our human tendency is to hoard wealth, but God calls us to resist this inclination and share with a generous hand. Most of us give from our abundance. This approach, however, doesn't require even a smidgen of faith.

If I only give what I can comfortably afford, without sacrifice, am I really giving generously? I saw a moving example of this as my team raised funds for a mission trip to Mexico. Some individuals gave one-time, substantial amounts, but almost every week one man tucked a small donation into our hands. We later discovered he was skipping lunch so he could donate his lunch money to our mission trip. Because he knew he could trust God to meet his needs, he was free to channel his blessings to others instead of hoarding them for himself.

When our team returned from Mexico, we showed pictures of the couples who had attended the marriage conference we presented. Then we shared how delighted our missionary friends were with the kitchen renovation our team had done. Next we shared how God had opened the door for us to lead a couple to the Lord who were on the verge of splitting up. By this time, the kind man who had donated his lunch money was smiling as broadly as we were.

"Hearing your stories and knowing I got to be a part of it brings me more joy than a hundred cheeseburger baskets," he said. He was experiencing the life that was truly life.

I've learned that spending money (or hoarding it) brings momentary delight. I've also learned, like my lunch-skipping friend, that denying temporary desires for the greater pleasures of eternity brings unimaginable joy.

Uncommon Thought

Generously investing in God's people and God's projects cracks open the door to the life that is truly life—one focused on eternity and guaranteed to last forever. This is true joy.

Unusual Faith

If you've never considered yourself rich, think again. Consider that true wealth has little to do with a bank account and everything to do with what God is doing on earth in people's lives.

Read 1 Timothy 6:6–19.

A Screamer's New Year

And the Lord's servant must not be quarrelsome
but must be kind to everyone, able to teach, not
resentful. Opponents must be gently instructed.

2 TIMOTHY 2:24–25

I come from a long line of screamers. My grandmother used to yell in Portuguese whenever she got angry. She broke dishes in a rubbish barrel when she got really mad. While we kids couldn't translate her fiery tirade, we certainly got the gist of it. Granny was mad, and everyone knew it.

The ability to scream in another language was lost on the second generation, so my mother just yelled. As teenagers, we knew when Mom's voice reached a certain volume, she meant business. It was time to get off our lazy bottoms and get moving.

I'd been well-schooled in the art of angry outbursts—and I was an excellent student. By the time my daughters were in elementary school, I'd perfected the art of loud, harsh, forceful outbursts. When I'd feel frustrated because my children weren't moving fast enough, I'd raise my voice.

Sometimes I'd blame my disposition on my Portuguese-Italian ethnicity. Other times I'd justify my explosive approach by saying, "It's just the way I was raised." I could rationalize every bark and growl—until that New Year's Day when God set me straight.

As is often the case at the start of a new year, I was feeling introspective. "Lord, I dedicate this year to you," I prayed. "Over the next twelve months, I want to become more like you. I want to please you in all that I do. Show me what you want me to do."

And then I paused. With pen in hand and journal ready, I waited to hear from God the nature of my assignment. Teach a Sunday school class? Volunteer at a crisis pregnancy center? Mentor a new believer? Before long, the still, small voice of the Holy Spirit whispered to me.

You aren't gentle.

"I know that, Lord, but I'm Portuguese. And Italian. Portuguese Italians yell a lot."

But Christians don't, the tender voice said. *You may be your mother's child, but you're also my child. And my children are gentle, peaceful, and full of self-control.*

Ouch.

Second Timothy 2:24–25 sums up God's words to me that day: "And the Lord's servant must not be quarrelsome but must be kind to everyone, able to teach, not resentful. Opponents must be gently instructed."

My New Year's Day exchange with the Lord began my journey toward gentleness. It's been a challenging trek. Decades of habits are hard to break. But looking back, I see three major steps:

Confess. The day I realized (and admitted) that I wasn't communicating in a God-honoring way was pivotal. For the first time, I saw my lack of gentleness through God's eyes, and I didn't excuse it. I stopped blaming my upbringing, ethnicity, and personality. Instead, I called it what it was—sin.

Repent. The second step in gaining victory over my lack of gentleness was to forsake it. The Bible calls this act *repentance.* When we repent, we're not just sorry for our sin or remorseful that we've gotten in trouble. We're genuinely broken. Our hearts hurt because we realize how much our behavior has offended God and wounded others. If we're truly repentant, we want to turn from our sin and allow God to change us.

Surrender. Sin usually involves a bit of pride, and my story is no exception. At first, I tried to "fix" myself. Every morning I determined to be gentle. And every day I failed. After many frustrating weeks, I realized I couldn't muster up gentleness. Only God could make me gentle. "Father, I can't do this on my own," I prayed. "I need your help."

Surrendering my pride enabled me to ask God to release His power into my struggle. I realized self-will and determination alone could never win this battle. Only God's power in me could give me the victory I craved. Whenever I felt anger and impatience rising up in me, I'd ask God for the self-control to respond gently instead. I looked up verses in the Bible that talked about gentleness, printed them out on index cards, and posted them in prominent places throughout the house. I memorized several and would quote them to myself when I felt my anger or frustration rising.

When I spoke harshly to my children or my husband, I'd ask for their forgiveness as soon as I realized it. Then I'd confess it to the

Lord and ask for His forgiveness. Every morning I'd pray, "Lord, make me gentler today than I was yesterday." Sometimes, when I really struggled, I'd ask a friend to hold me accountable.

Change didn't happen overnight. I'd make good progress, then I'd get sick or PMSy and bite off someone's head. When that happened, I'd return to what God had taught me. Confess. Repent. Surrender. Confess. Repent. Surrender.

Little by little my harsh words and impatient attitude softened into gentle words and patience. Twenty years later, I'm still not perfect, but I have changed. Sometimes when I share my story, people find it hard to believe I once was a screamer.

To God be the glory.

Uncommon Thought

Harshness seldom motivates. God is most glorified when we respond with gentleness.

Unusual Faith

If you were to ask your family, friends, or work associates to describe you, would they use the word *gentle*? Would God? If not, invite the Lord into your struggle. Confess your lack of gentleness. Repent of your anger and impatience. Surrender your disposition to the Lord, and ask Him to change it, one day at a time, for His glory.

Read 2 Timothy 2:22–26.

Thou Shalt Not . . . Pilfer?

Teach slaves to be subject to their masters in everything,
to try to please them, not to talk back to them, and
not to steal from them, but to show that they can
be fully trusted, so that in every way they will make
the teaching about God our Savior attractive.

TITUS 2:9–10

Jessie worked for an insurance firm downtown. On her lunch break, she used company stationary to write a letter to her cousin in prison. She tucked it into an envelope, ran it through the firm's postage meter, and sent it out with the afternoon mail.

Three weeks later the letter came back marked Return to Sender. The business manager opened it and promptly fired Jessie for unauthorized use of company stationery and petty theft.

"I didn't do anything wrong," Jessie insisted. "It's not really stealing. Everybody does it."

I thought of Jessie when I read Titus 2:9–10:

Teach slaves to be subject to their masters in everything, to try to please them, not to talk back to them, *and not to steal from them*, but to show that they can be fully trusted, so that in every way they will make the teaching about God our Savior attractive. (emphasis mine)

The New King James Version of the Bible uses the synonym *pilfer* in place of *steal*. *Pilfer* is a word we don't often hear these days, but it's a good one, one that more fully explains the essence of what Paul was teaching. Vocabulary.com defines *pilfer* in this way: "To pilfer is to steal something, typically of small value. Minor thefts, like taking a roll of toilet paper out of a public bathroom or napkins from the Early Bird Buffet are what your grandfather, for example, might pilfer."

Today's employees pilfer other things. In their article, "Hidden Cost of Office Pilfering," *Business Matters* lists the ten items employees most often steal from their employers: Post-it notes, tape, scissors, toilet paper, copy paper, USB memory sticks, notepads, pens, staplers, and highlighters.[14]

Like Jessie, 43 percent of the people who took an AOL job survey admitted to taking low-cost office supplies without thinking they're doing anything wrong. Others steal because they think their employers don't pay them enough or treat them well.[15]

Regardless of the motive or reasoning behind the action, the apostle Paul makes it clear that stealing of any kind is wrong. And he speaks on good authority—God's. In the eighth commandment, God clearly said, "You shall not steal" (Deuteronomy 5:19).

Any theft, whether it's a laptop or a Post-it note, is an offense in God's eyes. Paul reminded first-century Christians to be honest and above reproach in all their business dealings for several reasons.

First, stealing breaks man's law. Even the smallest theft is considered a misdemeanor and is punishable by law. Unless man's law contradicts God's law, Christians should always obey it.

Second, stealing undermines our employer's trust in us. Teddy Roosevelt once told a story of a ranch hand who rode with him on a cattle roundup. Coming upon some unbranded cows from another farm, the cowhand prepared to mark them with his ranch's brand. Roosevelt stopped him and sent him back to the ranch. "You're fired," he said. "If you'll steal *for* me, you'll steal *from* me."[16]

In contrast, when our employers "catch" us being honest, their confidence in our integrity grows. Paying for stamps, food, or services demonstrates that we're trustworthy and makes our employers more willing to trust us. An employee who refuses to steal time, money, or merchandise stands out in today's world.

Finally, stealing destroys our Christian witness. Let's take another look at Titus 2:9–10: "Teach slaves [employees] to be subject to their masters [employers] in everything, to try to please them, not to talk back to them, and not to steal from them, but to show that they can be fully trusted, *so that in every way they will make the teaching about God our Savior attractive*" (emphasis mine).

When a Christian embraces the standards of the world, the lowest common denominator, we harm the cause of Christ. Christian or non-Christian, employers know God's people shouldn't steal. They should be trustworthy and honest.

When we conduct ourselves with integrity in the workplace, we earn the right to talk about God. Our actions confirm rather than conflict with God's Word. Instead of being repelled by our hypocrisy, our employers and coworkers are attracted by the life we live every day.

I don't know if Jessie was a believer or not, but I know she was mistaken in thinking pilfering is okay. Whether "everybody's" doing it or not, God calls us to conduct ourselves with honesty and integrity. When we do, we'll have no fear of the law, we'll gain our employer's trust, and we'll earn the right to share our faith with our coworkers.

I'll take these treasures over a pilfered Post-it note any day, wouldn't you?

Uncommon Thought

When our actions align with what we believe, we make the teachings of Christ winsome and attractive.

Unusual Faith

In what areas have you been less than honest with your employer? Commit from now on to be above reproach in all that you do.

Read Titus 2:9–14.

Not Just What We Say

I am sending him—who is my very heart—back
to you. I would have liked to keep him with
me so that he could take your place in helping
me while I am in chains for the gospel.

PHILEMON 1:12–13

When was the last time you had to ask someone to do something difficult? Or talk with her about a sensitive subject? Or give him negative feedback?

Communication is challenging under any circumstances, but it's even dicier when we fear our message won't be well received. My friend Joy faced a situation that caused her to lie awake nights, stomach churning, trying to figure out how to approach a sticky subject.

"My Sunday school teacher said something in last week's lesson that just isn't biblical," she said one day over coffee. "It's serious enough that if she continues to teach it, people could really be led astray. But she's very sensitive and doesn't take correction well." Shaking her head, she continued. "I'm afraid to approach her, but I'm even more afraid to let her continue teaching something that's wrong. What am I supposed to do?"

Joy's problem is a common one. How do we communicate so

others will receive it? The tiny, one-chapter book of Philemon, tucked between the New Testament books of Titus and Hebrews, provides a guide.

Philemon is one of the many letters the apostle Paul wrote during his imprisonment. Named for its recipient, the letter describes Philemon as "our dear friend and fellow worker." A man of means, he owned at least one slave, Onesimus, who ran away. Somehow Onesimus met the apostle Paul, heard the gospel, and got saved. Paul lovingly describes Onesimus as one "who became my son while I was in chains" (v. 10).

Grateful to Paul for his transformed life, Onesimus served him faithfully during Paul's imprisonment. But Paul (and Onesimus) knew he needed to return to his master. "I am sending him—who is my very heart—back to you," Paul wrote to Philemon. "I would have liked to keep him with me so that he could take your place in helping me while I am in chains for the gospel" (vv. 12–13).

Onesimus deserved punishment for running away. But in light of his conversion to Christianity and transformed life, Paul hoped Philemon would forgive, release, and allow Onesimus to continue to serve him while in prison. It was a bold request, one Paul anticipated might not be well received.

So Paul, the master communicator, carefully crafted his letter. From his example, we can learn three steps to take when we have to communicate something difficult.

He affirmed Philemon. Paul wasn't currying favor by flattery or manipulation. He chose words that conveyed his genuine love and respect. "I always thank my God as I remember you in my prayers," he wrote, "because I hear about your love for all his holy people and your faith in the Lord Jesus. . . . Your love has given me great joy and encouragement, because you, brother, have refreshed the hearts of the Lord's people" (vv. 4–5, 7).

Affirming someone before we broach a sensitive subject reinforces our relationship and paves the way for the next step.

He spoke the "hard thing" with humility and respect. Paul had the apostolic right to demand Philemon to release Onesimus. Instead, he based his request on his faith and love. "Therefore, although in Christ I could be bold and order you to do what you ought to do, yet I prefer to appeal to you on the basis of love. It is as none other than Paul—an old man and now also a prisoner of Christ Jesus—that I appeal to you for my son Onesimus, who became my son while I was in chains. . . . I would have liked to keep him with me so that he could take your place in helping me while I am in chains for the gospel. But I did not want to do anything without your consent, so that any favor you do would not seem forced but would be voluntary" (vv. 8–10, 13–14).

Sometimes when we know we're right, it's easy to be arrogant and prideful. Carefully choosing our words and speaking them gently will determine, in large part, how they are received.

He affirmed his belief that Philemon would do the right thing. "Confident of your obedience, I write to you, knowing that you will do even more than I ask" (v. 21). Paul knew Philemon loved the Lord, so he challenged him to live out his faith and honor God by his decision. We can do the same by appealing to the good qualities we see in those we have to confront.

Following Paul's example, my friend Joy asked the Lord to help her share her concerns with her Sunday school teacher. She chose a time when they could talk uninterrupted and thanked her for the faithful way she prepared a lesson every week.

Then Joy expressed her concern. "I know you are committed to teaching the Word of God accurately," she said, "but I'm concerned about something you said in last week's lesson." She opened her Bible to the passage and explained her point of disagreement.

"I love you and value your teaching so much," she concluded. "Would you be willing to revisit this passage and tell me what you think after you've had time to study it further?"

Joy's Sunday school teacher thanked her for bringing the subject to her attention. "I don't know everything," she said, "and I certainly could be wrong about this. Let me do some study and we'll talk."

We don't know if Philemon agreed to release Onesimus back into Paul's care, but regardless of the outcome, Paul gave us a practical example of how to approach difficult subjects with humility and grace.

Uncommon Thought

When we have something hard to say, we can study God's Word and learn practical principles for successful communication.

Unusual Faith

Think back on the last conversation you had that didn't go as well as you'd hoped. How might the outcome have been different if you'd followed Paul's example? The next time you encounter a difficult conversation, commit to apply the principles Paul describes in the book of Philemon.

Read Philemon 1:1–25.

Who You Know

Let us then approach God's throne of grace with
confidence, so that we may receive mercy and
find grace to help us in our time of need.

HEBREWS 4:16

My friend Sam was in a pickle. He and his wife were days away from
a mission trip when they realized they didn't have a travel document
necessary to allow them to enter the country. He called my husband
and me in a panic, unsure what to do.

Eager to help, I blurted out the first thing that came to mind: "I
have a friend who's a judge. Maybe he can help."

A quick phone call confirmed that Clyde was, indeed, willing to
help. Unfortunately, being willing wasn't enough.

"I'm a family court judge," he said when I explained Sam's dilemma. "His request is out of my jurisdiction. I have no power."

Disappointed, I phoned Sam with the bad news. He thanked me
for trying, grateful I was willing to go to bat for him. "I've never
known anyone who had a judge's phone number in her contacts," he
said. "I'da been scared to death to call him."

Thankfully Sam's mission organization intervened. He received
the documents he needed, and he and his wife left for the mission

trip as scheduled. As I breathed a sigh of relief, I thought about my attempt to help him.

I wasn't afraid to phone Judge Clyde because I had a relationship with him. I was confident he'd listen carefully to my request and do everything within his power to help. Unfortunately, Clyde didn't have the power or the authority to intercede on Sam's behalf.

Hebrews 4:16 describes what I did: "Let us then approach God's throne of grace with confidence, so that we may receive mercy and find grace to help us in our time of need."

I called an important man to ask him to advocate on Sam's behalf because I had a relationship with him. How much more, then, should we feel the freedom to approach God, our Great High Priest, on the basis of our relationship with Him?

"We do not have a high priest who is unable to empathize with our weaknesses," Hebrews 4:15 says, "but we have one who has been tempted in every way, just as we are."

My friend Clyde empathized with Sam's predicament. Our friend Jesus empathizes with ours—our woes, our heartbreaks, our fears, our struggles, and our weaknesses. He, too, was tested and tempted, but because He was sinless, He earned the right not only to empathize but to advocate for us.

Judge Clyde didn't have the authority to act on Sam's behalf. His jurisdiction was limited and his power was narrow. Jesus Christ, however, has full jurisdiction and all power necessary to help us. We can trust Him, in faith, to be our provider and defender.

"Therefore," Hebrews 4:14 reminds us, "since we have a great high priest who has ascended into heaven, Jesus the Son of God, let us hold firmly to the faith we profess."

So the next time you face a situation that's bigger than you are and beyond your control, remember—it's all in Who you know.

Uncommon Thought

On the basis of our relationship with Jesus Christ, we can "approach God's throne of grace with confidence, so that we may receive mercy and find grace to help us in our time of need" (v. 16).

Unusual Faith

What are you struggling with today? Do you feel hindered, helpless, and hopeless? You may very well be, but God is not. Examine your heart and confess anything that might stand between you and God. Then approach Him boldly in prayer. On the basis of your relationship, confidently share your needs with Him. Trust that He'll receive your request with mercy and provide the help you need. Hold fast to your faith, knowing that God knows your needs and identifies with your struggles.

Read Hebrews 4:14–16.

The A I Couldn't Earn

For whoever keeps the whole law and yet stumbles
at just one point is guilty of breaking all of it.

JAMES 2:10

Dr. Cal Maddox was the hardest teacher in my high school.

Big, loud, and red-faced, he intimidated everyone. If his well-educated ear detected the slightest grammatical error in his students' speech, he'd yell, "Put it in," and we'd have to drop a penny into the Clemson Tiger fund.

Since most of us were USC Gamecock fans, we protested—loudly. It wasn't about the money. It was about the shame—the double shame of being caught and called out on a grammatical error and having to donate money—even one measly cent—to the Gamecocks' arch rival.

Dr. Maddox was equally alert to written grammatical errors. And spelling errors. And organizational errors. And usage errors. His goal was for us to be able to write a three-hundred-word essay in forty-five minutes with no mistakes.

I've always loved the ebb and flow of writing, so I eagerly embraced the thrill of Dr. Maddox's challenge. One day, about halfway through the first quarter, I looked over a recently graded writing assignment. I noticed with delight that the first page of my paper was free of his characteristic red marks. And so was the second. And the third.

Wonder of wonders, I'd written a paper with no spelling, grammatical, and usage errors! I'd accomplished Dr. Maddox's goal!

I flipped to the final page, eager to see my grade.

B.

B?

I'd written a paper completely free of spelling, grammatical, and usage errors, and I'd gotten a B?

"Dr. Maddox," I protested, "I think you made a mistake. You gave me a B instead of an A."

"It's not a mistake, Knuckle Head," he said in his no-nonsense voice. "Nobody gets an A in my class in the first quarter."

"Why not?"

"If I give you an A, then you'll have nothing to shoot for. You followed all the rules, but your paper isn't perfect. It can always be better."

By Dr. Maddox's standard, I reasoned, I'd never get an A. My writing would never be perfect. How would I ever achieve his impossible standard?

I thought of Dr. Maddox recently as I read James 2:10, "For whoever keeps the whole law and yet stumbles at just one point is guilty of breaking all of it." Jesus agreed with James's pronouncement. In the Sermon on the Mount, he declared, "Unless your righteousness surpasses that of the Pharisees and the teachers of the law, you will certainly not enter the kingdom of heaven" (Matthew 5:20).

God, like Dr. Maddox, set forth an impossible standard—perfection. The law He gave to the Israelites through Moses demanded obedience to more than six hundred commandments if the Israelites wanted to receive eternal life. Although thousands of years have passed, the standard remains unchanged. If we want to go to heaven, we must be perfect.

Are you feeling as hopeless as I did that day I discovered Dr. Maddox's requirement for an A?

Good, because this is where things begin to look up.

In 2 Corinthians 5:21 we are told of the great provision God made for us through Jesus Christ. "God made him who had no sin to be sin for us, so that in him we might become the righteousness of God."

Because of our sinful nature, we can never satisfy the stringent requirements of the law. All it takes is one sin to make us a sinner: one wrong thought, one wrong action, one good deed we should have done but failed to do. Even if we commit only one sin a day (and who can manage to sin only once a day?), over a lifetime we'll have committed more than 75,000 sins.

But Christ, the God-man, satisfied all six hundred requirements of the law by living a perfect, sinless life. Because He had no sin of His own to die for, He could pay the sin debt for us—for you and for me.

We deserve to die for our sins and spend eternity separated from God. Jesus chose to die in our place, satisfying God's wrath and giving us His righteousness. He earned the A, and when I placed my faith in Christ, God wrote His A on my report card.

The key to eternal life and a relationship with God isn't trying harder. It's giving up. Giving up our efforts to earn God's favor. Giving up our self-righteousness. Receiving Christ's righteousness. Giving up our pride and self-sufficiency, throwing ourselves at God's feet, and crying, "God, have mercy on me, a sinner."

"If you declare with your mouth, 'Jesus is Lord,' and believe in your heart that God raised him from the dead, you will be saved. For it is with your heart that you believe and are justified, and it is with your mouth that you profess your faith and are saved. As Scripture says, 'Anyone who believes in him will never be put to shame'" (Romans 10:9–11).

Through hard work and creativity, I eventually earned an A in Dr. Maddox's class. Through Christ's sacrificial death on the cross, He earned the A I need to enter heaven. And then He offered it to me.

As my pastor Dick Lincoln used to say, "I didn't earn it. I don't deserve it. But I am infinitely grateful."

Uncommon Thought

None can ever say, "It was too hard to get to heaven." Everything God required, Christ provided through His death on the cross.

Unusual Faith

Christ offers salvation to "everyone who calls on the name of the Lord" (Acts 2:21). Have you accepted His offer? If not, why not? Why not trust Him today? If you've taken this all-important faith step, take some time today to reflect on this amazing gift.

Read James 4:6–10.

Why Is Life So Hard?

Dear friends, do not be surprised at the fiery
ordeal that has come on you to test you, as though
something strange were happening to you.

1 PETER 4:12

I remember sitting in Bible study one day as a young adult. I'd only been married a few years. My husband and I had two young children, good jobs, and a satisfying ministry. Life was good.

When the Bible study leader raised the subject of suffering and quoted 1 Peter 4:12, I struggled to relate. When she cross-referenced Jesus's words to His followers, "In this world you will have trouble," I raised my hand.

"Is this an absolute?" I asked. "Because I can't really say I've experienced suffering or trouble. Does this mean that if I haven't suffered, I'm not a Christian?"

A shadow flickered in her eyes, hinting at the truth I knew was coming. "No, it doesn't mean you're not a Christian. It means your trouble hasn't come yet."

And she was right. In the years since, my family and I have experienced significant trials. We've lost loved ones—three siblings in one year. We've walked through marital challenges, unemployment, depression, injury, the heartbreak of shattered dreams, and painful ministry struggles. Life has been hard, and many days/weeks/months/years haven't been easy.

Are you depressed yet? Did the apostle Peter write his first book to frighten and discourage believers? Not at all. He wrote to men and women of the early church to speak truth and hope into their hardships. While my life has been challenging, and I suspect yours has, too, most of our trials can't compare to the experiences of the first-century believers.

Displaced from their beloved Jerusalem, where they had enjoyed deep, sweet fellowship with the church that sprang from Christ's death and resurrection, they now feared for their lives. Persecution dogged their days and stalked their nights. Emperor Nero unleashed an all-out attack on Christians, covering many of them in pitch and using them as human torches to light his gardens. For sport, he fed believers to the lions while spectators cheered.

And we think we've got it rough.

But we do. Our lives are hard. Not lion-eating, torch-burning hard, but hard nonetheless.

When our trials come, Peter reminds us that we shouldn't be surprised. Jesus, the sinless Savior whose only purpose was to rescue humanity from sin and ourselves, suffered in unimaginable ways. His mission was pure, good, and without question, yet He was despised and rejected by men, a man of sorrows, and acquainted with grief. Yet because He suffered on the cross, we won't have to suffer for our sins in eternity. His suffering had a purpose and, in a small way, our suffering in this world gives us a glimpse of what Jesus experienced on our behalf.

Yet somehow we continue to expect that life should be easy. That trials are abnormal and an indication that something is wrong. Trials aren't abnormal, but they do remind us that something is wrong. Our world is damaged—by sin, sickness, and death. When we expect it to be otherwise, we set up an unattainable standard that has the power to steal our joy and faith. If we anticipate life will be easy, then whenever it isn't, we wonder, why has God failed me? Doesn't He care? How can He love me and still allow this?

But when we understand life is hard, then we're not surprised. Instead, we can face our situation with faith, trust, and even hope.

As a new mother, I remember talking with a seasoned mom shortly after our daughter's birth. "She cries so much," I said.

"Of course she does," she replied. "She's a baby. Babies cry. But it will get better, I promise."

I can imagine a similar conversation with Peter. "Life is so hard," I'd say.

"Of course it is," he'd reply. "The world is broken. Broken worlds are hard. But it will get better, I promise."

If life is hard for you right now, don't be surprised. Take comfort in the knowledge that Jesus isn't just walking with you, He's walking ahead of you—into every moment and every day. And while our days on earth will be filled with challenges, I suspect the hardships of this world will make the ease of the next that much sweeter. Because this world is not our home, we can face our trials with hope.

"Dear friends, do not be surprised at the fiery ordeal that has come on you to test you, as though something strange were happening to you. But rejoice inasmuch as you participate in the sufferings of Christ, so that you may be overjoyed when his glory is revealed" (1 Peter 4:12–13).

Uncommon Thought

We live in a broken world filled with broken people. Life is hard, and it will continue to be hard as long as we walk this ball of earth. To expect otherwise is unrealistic, naive, and dangerous.

Unusual Faith

The next time a hard situation enters your life, instead of wallowing in shock and dismay, respond with faith and hope. Say, "Life *is* hard, and while this situation has caught me by surprise, it hasn't surprised God. I choose to trust Him to lead, guide, and provide all I need." Then watch what He does in and through you.

Read 1 Peter 4:12–19.

Sowing Faith Seeds

And I will make every effort to see that after my departure
you will always be able to remember these things.

2 PETER 1:15

If Wall Street measured spiritual wealth, my childhood portfolio was
a bust.

Unlike many of my friends who were second, third, or even
fourth generation Christians, I wasn't reared in a spiritual home. Santa
sat right next to baby Jesus on the Christmas mantle. Our church at-
tendance was spotty. And no one ever explained how Jesus fit into my
Easter basket with the chocolate eggs and jelly beans.

But as I look back on my early years, there were a few deposits in
my spiritual bank account.

One day my dad sketched the story of Noah and the flood. The
story and stick figure drawings fascinated me. I'd never heard the
story before. I had no idea it was true, nor that it came from the Bible.

When I was six, I attended Vacation Bible School with a friend.
A week later the minister and two blue-haired ladies knocked on our
door. They presented me with a black King James Version Bible.
On the inside someone had neatly inscribed my name and written a
verse—John 3:16. For many years, it was the only Bible in our home.

I often spent the weekends with my Portuguese grandmother.

Granny didn't go to church, but she prayed her rosary every night. Lying beside her as I drifted off to sleep, I'd hear her whispering the words to the Lord's Prayer. One morning she taught me to recite the Twenty-Third Psalm. I didn't understand most of it, but I repeated the words until I could say it flawlessly. To this day I don't know how she learned it, but I've never forgotten that early-morning lesson.

I thought of my paltry nest egg of spiritual assets when I read the three-chapter book of 2 Peter.

"So I will always remind you of these things," the aged apostle wrote to his spiritual children, "even though you know them and are firmly established in the truth you now have. I think it is right to refresh your memory as long as I live in the tent of this body, because I know that I will soon put it aside, as our Lord Jesus Christ has made clear to me. And I will make every effort to see that after my departure you will always be able to remember these things" (2 Peter 1:12–15).

God had revealed to Peter that his death was imminent. The bold apostle had survived much persecution for his faith, but now the day of his departure was at hand. As many do when they know their lives are ending, Peter wanted to leave a legacy for his children—an inheritance to ensure their future success.

But unlike many who bequeathed houses, businesses, and land, Peter wasn't concerned with leaving a financial legacy. He wanted to leave a *spiritual* legacy.

I want to leave a spiritual legacy for my children too. I want to make every effort for my children (both biological and spiritual) to remember the truths I based my life on. Whether or not we have children of our own, we should all be investing in and discipling someone younger than us. Especially young believers who didn't grow up in a Christian home.

How do we disciple others? Here are a few ideas:

Memorize Scripture and teach it to others. When we hide God's Word in our hearts, He promises it will *always* accomplish the purpose He has for it. When my children were young, I selected important passages of Scripture like the Ten Commandments and the Beatitudes and printed them out. As we drove across town to swim team practice and music lessons, we'd alternate reading the verses aloud and reciting them. Before long we'd committed several long passages and key verses to memory. If you're working with an adult, memorize key passages together.

Personalize a One Year Bible *for someone.* As you read through the Bible, write notes, insights, and prayers in the margins. Claim promises in prayer for them and note the date you prayed. As you read the prayers recorded by the psalmists, prophets, and kings, personalize them with their name and pray them on their behalf. Then make a note.When you reach the end of the Bible, present it on a special occasion (birthday, graduation, marriage) as a gift. I gave a Bible to each of my daughters on their sixteenth birthdays.

Live a life of integrity and authenticity. You don't have to be perfect—only Jesus never sinned—but you do have to be humble and transparent. If you sin, confess it, repent of it, and ask whomever you sinned against to forgive you. Stand for what's right even when it costs you. Don't compromise your convictions. Speak the truth in love. Extend hospitality. Give generously. Make worship and Bible study a priority.

Keep a journal. Like the apostle Peter, write down meaningful Bible verses, truths you've learned about God, and answers to prayers. Write prayers for your loved ones, recording promises and the hope God gives you. Compose psalms of praise.

When Peter died, he left behind a legacy of Scripture, wise counsel, faith, and authenticity that has influenced countless generations. We can do the same.

Uncommon Thought

If we, like Peter, intentionally sow seeds of faith into others, the effects of our lives can ripple on into eternity long after we're gone.

Unusual Faith

Think about the people in your life you'd most like to influence for eternity. They may be biological children, spiritual children, or younger women who need a spiritual mentor. You don't have to be a biblical scholar to invest in someone else's life. Be yourself and share your genuine love for God and His Word. Trust the Holy Spirit to lead you. Ask God which of the ideas above (or one of your own) would be the best way to sow seeds of faith into their lives, then take the first step. Begin today.

Read 2 Peter 1:12–21.

1 JOHN

Fellowship and Fish Tacos

We proclaim to you what we have seen and heard, so
that you also may have fellowship with us. And our
fellowship is with the Father and with his Son, Jesus
Christ. We write this to make our joy complete.

1 JOHN 1:3–4

My friend Becky and I were driving from Columbia, South Carolina, to Wilmington, Delaware, to attend a friend's wedding. As we approached the beltway that would take us around Washington, DC, I reminisced about the last time I'd been in the area.

"I was visiting my daughter, and she told me about this taco place across the street from her apartment. She said, 'Mom, you *have* to try the fish tacos. They are aMAzing.' Well, fish tacos sounded pretty disgusting, but she went on and on about them, so I finally agreed to try them."

"And did you like them?" Becky asked.

"They were the most delicious tacos I'd ever put in my mouth," I said. "We went to the restaurant three times that weekend because I enjoyed them so much."

"Yum," she said, "I've never had fish tacos, but after your description, I think I'd like to try them."

243

We drove a while in silence.

"Hey, Becky."

"Yeah?"

"It wouldn't be that out of the way to swing by Alexandria on our way north," I said.

"Are you thinking what I'm thinking?"

"That we could stop at District Taco, and you could try the fish tacos?"

"YES!" she said. "Let's do it."

The book of 1 John begins with a rave review similar to the one I gave Becky about fish tacos. Only the apostle John wasn't gushing over lightly-seasoned grilled fish with mango slaw. He was describing his experiences with Jesus.

"We've seen Him, and touched Him, and heard Him speak," he wrote. "We've experienced the dramatic change Christ makes in a person's life, and we want to tell you about it. It's too wonderful not to share."

And then he wrote, with a heart filled with love for God and for those to whom he was writing, "We are writing these things so that *our joy may be complete*" (1:4, HCSB, emphasis mine).

It wasn't enough for John and his fellow believers to experience Jesus for themselves. They knew sharing Him with others would bring them even greater joy—a joy that was fully complete.

Fish tacos pale in comparison to the deliciousness of walking with Jesus. However when Becky and I sat across from each other, unwrapped our food, and bit into our tacos, our shared experience was ten times better than if we'd eaten them alone. I loved them, and now, so did she. Sharing joy with someone multiplies it.

The same is true with our salvation and the day-to-day experiences of the Christian life. When we share what God is doing in our lives, and it resonates with someone else, our experiences become richer. Inviting Christ into the conversation creates a heavenly circle of fellowship with God in our midst.

And yet, it's a curious thing. When believers gather, they usually talk about family, work, relationships, and hobbies—everything but Jesus. Sharing these aspects of our lives is fun, but if we limit our conversation to these topics, we miss the sweetest topic of all—what Jesus is doing in our lives.

After our bellies were full of fish tacos and mango slaw, Becky and I climbed back into the car for the last leg of our trip. Soon our conversation turned to matters of faith. We shared joys and struggles, happiness and hurts. We talked about what God was teaching us through His Word and what we hoped to see Him do in the future. The miles disappeared under our wheels as we bragged on God and what He was doing in our lives. Before we realized it, our destination was in sight.

I wonder if this is also the best way to log the miles of our lives—walking with God and sharing Him with others. With God in the midst, as the apostle John wrote, our joy will be complete.

Uncommon Thought

When we step out on a conversational ledge and talk about spiritual things, our fellowship with each other and with God becomes much deeper and richer.

Unusual Faith

The next time you gather with believers, share something God is teaching you. Tell how God has revealed himself to you or describe how you've seen evidence of His care for you. Not everyone will want to talk about spiritual things, but some will. Watch how these conversations deepen your relationships with each other and make your joy complete.

Read 1 John 1:1–4.

Itchy and Scratchy

It has given me great joy to find some of your children
walking in the truth, just as the Father commanded us.

2 JOHN 1:4

Their names were Itchy and Scratchy, and they were our forefathers.
They lived in caves, grunted, and had ape-like facial features and mar-
ginal intelligence.

When I encountered this description of the first humans in one
of my children's school books, I marched it to the trash can. As a
Christian, I believe the biblical account of creation, which includes a
detailed description of how God created Adam and Eve, the first man
and woman. While the book of Genesis doesn't mention if our early
ancestors lived in caves, it does mention that, from the very beginning,
they were intelligent, articulate beings. Adam named and classified all
the animals God created, something Itchy and Scratchy could never
do. It was obvious from the first few pages of the book I held that the
author didn't believe the biblical account of creation.

Halfway to the trash can, however, I stopped. Earlier that morning I had read the book of 2 John during my quiet time. Comprised
of one chapter and only thirteen verses, John's letter to an unnamed
lady uses the word *truth* five times in the first four verses. Verse 4 says

this, "It has given me great joy to find some of your children walking in the truth, just as the Father commanded us."

John was referring, of course, to the truth of Scripture. In a day when the fundamentals of the faith were being attacked, John had written the letter to urge these fellow believers to base their lives on the truth of God's Word.

I realized then that while it was important to have accurate, biblical books as the foundation of my children's education, it was also important that my daughters knew how to counteract lies with biblical truth.

Instead of chucking the book in the trash, I opened the Bible to Genesis and read the story of creation to them. Then I read the account of Itchy and Scratchy. "We know God's Word is true," I said, "so let's compare this story with the Bible and see if the author's telling the truth." With a little guidance, my daughters successfully separated the truth from the lies in the story of Itchy and Scratchy.

If I'd thrown the book away, I'd have missed a valuable teaching opportunity to strengthen my daughters' faith and teach them how to process information through the grid of Scripture. While I still believe the majority of our children's textbooks should have a biblical worldview, I realized that day that I could use the occasional secular book or movie to train my children to apply biblical truth.

Even if no children live in your home, the little book of 2 John reminds us that, as Christians, we should hold up everything we hear, watch, or read to the plumb line of Scripture. Otherwise, worldly (and even demonic) philosophies can muddy our thinking and cause us to embrace lies. Popular culture is very persuasive.

If we don't fill our minds with biblical truth, it's easy to be deceived. Reading good books, watching inspiring movies, and listening to Christian music can help. The most valuable way to learn truth, however, is to read the Bible every day. I've often discovered the answer to a question or problem I've been struggling with when I read my Bible.

Before you open the Word, however, pray and ask the Holy Spirit to help you understand what you're reading. Then, after you read a passage of Scripture, jot down what's most meaningful to you. It could be something you learned about God, an instruction to apply to your life, or a promise to claim. Writing it down helps cement the truths in our minds and gives us notes to refer back to later. Before long you'll have a precious record of God's conversations with you.

In the Bible, we have the truth our world needs. As we move through each day, we must listen with discernment and filter everything through the absolute grid of Scripture. As we learn God's Word, we can apply His wisdom to our life and share it with others. Through the power of Scripture, we can change the world, one truth at a time.

Uncommon Thought
Our world is searching for truth while truth sits right here in front of us.

Unusual Faith
Today, compare what you hear in conversation and through the media with the truth of God's Word. Challenge the lies by sharing what you heard with someone.

Read 2 John 1:1–13.

Is Your Soul Prospering?

Beloved, I pray that you may prosper in all things
and be in health, just as your soul prospers.

3 John 1:2 (NKJV)

My friend Sue was about as sick as anyone I'd ever seen. Five months into her battle with pancreatic cancer, her body was ravaged by both the disease and her doctors' valiant attempts to cure her. She hadn't eaten in weeks, and her abdomen was distended because of fluid buildup. Every breath was an effort. She spent most days lying in a recliner in her sunroom. In the hospital more often than she was home, Sue's tumor markers were rising. Doctors said her body wasn't strong enough to endure another round of aggressive chemotherapy. She knew things weren't looking good.

I stopped by her home one spring afternoon, planning to pray with her and speak some words of encouragement. Instead, my dear, sick friend encouraged me. She later shared some of her thoughts in a CaringBridge blog post: "I'm just holding my Lord's hand and letting Him lead me through each day. I don't know where we're going, but He does."

She shared Isaiah 40:31: "Those who wait on the LORD shall renew their strength; they shall mount up with wings like eagles, they shall run and not be weary, they shall walk and not be faint" (NKJV).

"I trust God to follow through on this and all His promises," she wrote. "It's what I cling to with a vivid image of swooping over green hills and winding blue rivers, lifted by divine wings. It's where that one river will take me that makes me unafraid now. He's winged me successfully through many procedures and surgeries because of cancer, which has drawn me closer than I've ever been to Him. Is cancer a blessing? In more ways than you can imagine. Even bone-thin, too weak to push back my recliner, and dreading each procedure . . . I still count it all joy."

I thought of my friend, Sue, now safely home with the Lord, when I read the first lines of the tiny book of 3 John. One of the last books of the Bible, 3 John contains a brief letter from the apostle John to his dear friend and spiritual son, Gaius.

"Beloved," John wrote, "I pray that you may prosper in all things and be in health, just as your soul prospers" (1:2).

More than material comforts or good health, John knew the greatest gift Gaius could obtain was a prosperous soul.

What does a prosperous soul look like? In many ways, it has the same qualities as a prosperous bank account: riches, reach, and rewards.

A prosperous bank account has riches in cash. A prosperous soul has riches in love, joy, peace, patience, kindness, goodness, faithfulness, gentleness, and self-control (Galatians 5:22–23).

A prosperous bank account has reach. It has the power to impact and influence others' lives through financial, philanthropic, and charitable gifts. A prosperous soul has the ability to reach beyond the earthly sphere into the heavenly realms. It partners with God to share the power of Christ to redeem and change lives forever.

A prosperous bank account has rewards. Its investments pay dividends, which are then reinvested, again and again. A prosperous soul gains its rewards by giving away, leveraging God's upside-down economy to become spiritually rich. As the prosperous soul sows seeds of love, charity, and good deeds on this earth, its cache of heavenly rewards grows ever greater.

Sue taught me that even when our health is poor, we can still be spiritually rich. The same famine that makes us spiritually hungry can drive us to seek out the spiritual food that can deeply satisfy our cravings.

If you're feeling a little soul-starved today, why not pull up a chair to God's banquet table? Seek God's presence in prayer and Bible reading. As you gather close, He'll feed you with a generous hand and a welcoming heart. Like my friend Sue, I pray your soul will richly prosper today.

Uncommon Thought

A "famine" can strip us of our abundance of relationships, resources, or significance. It can also cause us to hungrily seek the abundant feast our souls crave and Christ offers.

Unusual Faith

Is your soul prospering? If not, commit to spend time with God in prayer and Bible reading this week. Ask Him to fill your hungering soul as only He can do.

Read 3 John 1:1–14.

Standing before Jesus

To him who is able to keep you from stumbling
and to present you before his glorious presence
without fault and with great joy—to the only
God our Savior be glory, majesty, power and
authority, through Jesus Christ our Lord.

JUDE 1:24–25

What will it be like to stand before Jesus?

Regardless of how or when we die, there will come a day when each of us will come face to face with Jesus Christ. Imagine for a moment what that will look like.

The Old Testament tells us about a few men who saw manifestations of God and lived to tell about it. Jacob saw God and was thankful God spared his life (Genesis 32:30). Moses saw God, hid his face, and feared to look at Him (Exodus 3:6). The Israelites saw the thunder, lightning, and smoke that accompanied God's presence and trembled in fear. "Speak to us yourself and we will listen," they said to Moses. "But do not have God speak to us or we will die" (Exodus 20:19). So Moses went alone. Afterward, the Israelites were so overwhelmed by the glory that shone from Moses's face that they begged him to cover it with a veil.

Isaiah saw God, "high and lifted up," the train of His robe filling

the temple. "Woe to me!" he cried. "I am ruined! For I am a man of
unclean lips, and I live among a people of unclean lips, and my eyes
have seen the King, the LORD Almighty" (Isaiah 6:5).

When I picture myself standing before Him, I don't picture
standing at all. I imagine myself as a blubbery, slobbery, laid-out, face-
down-on-the-floor puddle. One look into the eyes that can see past
my skin and into my soul, and my knees will fail me. One glimpse of
the nail prints in His hands, and I'll be flat on my face.

Ground-level will place me eye-level at Jesus's feet. I'll see more
of the bruised flesh and jagged wounds He suffered for me, and my
heart will crack in two.

Christ's purity—the whiter-than-snow brilliance of His perfection—will shame me. My sinfulness—the filthy rags of my "righteousness"—will undo me.

"I'm not worth it," I'll sob as the spear in His side vicariously
pierces mine. "I'm not worth it. I don't deserve this kind of love."

If you, like I, feel a profound sense of unworthiness, God has
placed verses like the second-to-last in the one-chapter book of Jude
to give us hope.

"To him who is able to keep you from stumbling and to present
you before his glorious presence *without fault* and *with great joy*" (v. 24,
emphasis mine).

Without fault—"There is now no condemnation for those who are
in Christ Jesus" Romans 8:1 reminds us. No guilt. No fear. No sure
and certain punishment for the thousands of ways we've failed Him.

With great joy—"Though you have not seen him, you love him;
and even though you do not see him now, you believe in him and are
filled with an inexpressible and glorious joy, for you are receiving the
end result of your faith, the salvation of your souls," 1 Peter 1:8–9

says. Pure, unadulterated, emancipating joy will fill our spirits, banishing shame, remorse, and regret forever.

"Do you love me?" Jesus may ask, as He asked Peter that day on the shore.

"Lord, you know I do," we'll say.

Then He'll raise us to our feet, look deep into our eyes, and wrap His big, strong arms around us. With the bear hug of the millennium, He will squeeze our heartbreak away.

"Welcome home," He'll say. "I've been waiting for you."

Uncommon Thought
If I've placed my faith in Christ alone for my salvation, I will one day stand before God faultless and with great joy.

Unusual Faith
How do you imagine your first encounter with Christ? Close your eyes and picture it. Will you cry, cringe, or celebrate? Now spend a few minutes meditating (thinking deeply) on the verses in this devotion. Allow the truth of God's Word to enhance your vision of what it's going to be like when you see Jesus face to face. And then live today like you believe it.

Read Jude 1:20–25.

REVELATION

Revelation's Special Blessing

Blessed is the one who reads aloud the words of
this prophecy, and blessed are those who hear
it and take to heart what is written in it.

REVELATION 1:3

If one of my neighbors had looked out her window one crisp winter morning, she would have been concerned at best and alarmed at worst. She would have seen me, dressed in athletic clothes, walking briskly down the road. A white cord connected ear buds to the iPhone in my pocket.

This isn't unusual. I walk my neighborhood almost every morning. If she looked closely, however, she'd have seen that I was crying. Great big crocodile tears.

And if she lingered a little longer at the window, she would have seen that not only was I crying, I was also smiling. Really big—in a teary sort of way. Now that's beyond concerning.

Revelation 1:3 explains what was happening that morning: "Blessed is the one who reads aloud the words of this prophecy, and blessed are those who hear it and take to heart what is written in it."

Some mornings I have time to linger over my daily Bible reading. If I'm working from home, I pour myself a cup of tea, curl up with my Bible, and read and pray. On days I work outside the home, however, I multitask. Instead of choosing between spending time in God's Word or exercising, I do both. I lace up my tennis shoes, stick my ear buds in my ears, and listen to that day's reading on my Bible app.

By the time I've completed the circle of my neighborhood, I've listened to at least two chapters of the Old Testament, a chapter in the New Testament, a Psalm, and a Proverb.

That morning I had only one book left to complete my reading—Revelation. As the narrator's rich tenor voice filled my ears, I was transported far beyond the cul de sacs and avenues of my neighborhood to the third heaven, where God the Father sat on the throne.

"And I saw a mighty angel proclaiming in a loud voice, 'Who is worthy to break the seals and open the scroll?' But no one in heaven or on earth or under the earth could open the scroll or even look inside it. I wept and wept because no one was found who was worthy to open the scroll or look inside." (Revelation 5:2–4)

I heard John's despair in the narrator's voice. I felt his hopelessness as he realized no one was worthy to open the scroll. My heart broke to imagine the aged apostle crumpled in a heap at the foot of God's throne. Like John, I wept.

But then the narrator's voice changed. Despair gave way to excitement.

"Do not weep! See, the Lion of the tribe of Judah, the Root of David, has triumphed. He is able to open the scroll and its seven seals."

Then his voice changed once again. Holy awe added to his excitement.

> "Then I saw a Lamb, looking as if it had been slain, standing at the center of the throne, encircled by the four living creatures and the elders. . . . He went and took the scroll from the right hand of him who sat on the throne. And when he had taken it, the four living creatures and the twenty-four elders fell down before the Lamb. . . .
>
> "And they sang a new song, saying: 'You are worthy to take the scroll and to open its seals, because you were slain, and with your blood you purchased for God persons from every tribe and language and people and nation.'"

The narrator's voice, if possible, grew wider, and broader, and deeper. It spanned the expanse of heaven and filled my mind and heart with John's vision.

> "Then I looked and heard the voice of many angels, numbering thousands upon thousands, and ten thousand times ten thousand. They encircled the throne and the living creatures and the elders. In a loud voice they were saying: 'Worthy is the Lamb, who was slain, to receive power and wealth and wisdom and strength and honor and glory and praise!'" (vv. 5–9, 11–12)

My face split in a joyous grin while tears of joy poured down my cheeks. Anyone looking out her window that day as I walked down the street would have wondered what in the world was wrong with me.

I'd read the words of Revelation many times, but that morning, hearing the narrator describe the sights and sounds of heaven, the passage came alive like it never had before. I laughed. I cried. I rejoiced. Somewhere between Heartwood Circle and Red Leaf Lane, I caught a glimpse of what we have to look forward to in heaven, and I was overwhelmed.

"Blessed is the one who reads aloud the words of this prophecy," God promises, and so it was for me that day.

Uncommon Thought

Beyond our sight are wonders few have glimpsed this side of eternity. Perhaps this is why God chose to end the Bible with a sneak preview—to give us hope and encourage us to press on.

Unusual Faith

Have you ever read aloud or listened to someone read aloud the book of Revelation? Today read Revelation 21 and 22 aloud. Or, even better, listen to them on an audio Bible app on your phone or computer. BibleGateway is an excellent source. As the narrator reads, imagine all of forever in the presence of God. No sickness. No pain. No sorrow. Best of all, picture Jesus wrapping His arms around you and welcoming you home. Let the hope of this meeting inspire and encourage you.

Read Revelation 21–22.

Notes

1. Kenneth Gangel provides great insight into Caleb and offers a list of "three factors working against" Caleb's commitment and dedication. I have borrowed from and expounded on his list found in *Holman Old Testament Commentary: Joshua* (Nashville: Broadman & Holman, 2002), 213.
2. Gangel, *Holman Old Testament Commentary: Joshua*, 213.
3. Joni Eareckson Tada, "God Permits What He Hates," *Joni and Friends*, May 15, 2013, https://www.joniandfriends.org /radio/4-minute/god-permits-what-he-hates1/.
4. Carol Kent, "Kent's Story," Speak Up for Hope, http://speak upforhope.org/h/1/kents-story/.
5. J. Barton Payne, *Encyclopedia of Biblical Prophecy* (New York: Harper & Row, 1973), quoted in Wayne Jackson, "How Many Prophecies Are in the Bible," ChristianCourier.com, https:// www.christiancourier.com/articles/318-how-many-prophecies -are-in-the-bible.
6. "Hope and Optimism," Positive Psychology News, http:// positivepsychologynews.com/image-maps/positive-emotions /hope-and-optimism (February 27, 2018).
7. William B. Nelson Jr., *Baker's Evangelical Dictionary of Biblical Theology*, ed. Walter A. Elwell, s.v. "Hope" (Grand Rapids: Baker, 1996), https://www.biblestudytools.com/dictionaries /bakers-evangelical-dictionary/hope.html (February 27, 2018).
8. Charles R. Swindoll, "Hope Beyond the Hurt," Insight for

Living Ministries, June 15, 2009, http://www.insight.org
/resources/article-library/individual/hope-beyond-the-hurt.

9. Abby Johnson, "September 7, 2013," Abby Johnson (blog),
October 20, 2013, http://www.abbyjohnson.org/abby
johnson/september-7-2013.

10. John MacArthur, *The MacArthur Daily Bible* (Nashville: Thomas
Nelson, 2003), 848.

11. Oswald Chambers, *My Utmost for His Highest: An Updated Edition in Today's Language* (Grand Rapids: Discovery House, 1992),
June 25.

12. Ruth Alexander, "Dollar Benchmark: The Rise of the
$1-a-Day Statistic," *BBC News*, March 9, 2012, https://
www.bbc.co.uk/news/magazine-17312819.

13. Catherine Rampell, "The Haves and the Have-Nots," *New York
Times*, January 31, 2011, https://economix.blogs.nytimes
.com/2011/01/31/the-haves-and-the-have-nots/.

14. "Hidden Cost of Office Pilfering," *Business Matters*, May 20,
2012, http://www.bmmagazine.co.uk/news/hidden-cost-of
-office-pilfering/.

15. Barbara Safani, "What's Considered Stealing at Work?" Aol
.com, January 27, 2011, https://www.aol.com/2011/01/27
/whats-considered-stealing-at-work/.

16. Theodore Roosevelt, "At Kansas City, MO, May 1, 1903,"
*A Compilation of the Messages and Speeches of Theodore Roosevelt,
1901–1905*, ed. Alfred Henry Lewis (Washington, DC: Bureau
of National Literature and Art, 1906), 317.

About the Author

Lori Hatcher fell in love with books sitting on her father's lap when she was two years old. Every week they'd go to the grocery store, where he'd help her choose a new Little Golden book. Then he'd read it to her until she could recite it perfectly.

She fell in love with God's Word as an eighteen-year-old college student trying to do everything "right." Since 1982, she's been on a grand adventure of digging into the Bible. In the process, she's also fallen madly in love with her Savior.

Now she's an empty-nester who lives with her pastor-husband delightfully close to their four grandchildren in Lexington, South Carolina. She edits a regional Christian magazine, blogs, and writes for publications such as *Guideposts, War Cry, The Old Schoolhouse, Today's Christian Living,* and *Christian Living in the Mature Years.* Her other job as a dental hygienist provides an unlimited supply of material (names changed, of course), but her daily time in God's Word helps her connect life experiences with eternal truth.

A perfect day would include praying with her husband, walking three miles in the sunshine, eating food she didn't have to cook, laughing with her grandchildren, and writing undisturbed while all four of them napped beside her in the mountains or at the beach. This, she hopes, is what heaven will be like.

If you enjoyed *Refresh Your Faith,* Lori would be so grateful if you'd post an honest review on Amazon. Nothing fancy, just tell folks what you liked about it.

For more five-minute devotions, connect with Lori on her blog, *Hungry for God . . . Starving for Time* (www.LoriHatcher.com), on Facebook (Hungry for God), Twitter (@Lori Hatcher2), and Pinterest (Hungry for God).

Help us get the word out!

Our Daily Bread Publishing exists to feed the soul with the Word of God.

If you appreciated this book, please let others know.

- Pick up another copy to give as a gift.
- Share a link to the book or mention it on social media.
- Write a review on your blog, on a bookseller's website, or at our own site (ourdailybreadpublishing.org).
- Recommend this book for your church, book club, or small group.

Connect with us:

 @ourdailybread

@ourdailybread

@ourdailybread

Our Daily Bread Publishing
PO Box 3566
Grand Rapids, Michigan 49501 USA

 books@odb.org